T0276694

Euro
&
The Architect

Europe
'The most important playwright to have emerged north of the
Border in years. *Europe* is a fierce, compassionate, mighty
ambitious drama . . . there is the sharp, analytic intelligence,
the crackling inventiveness of a real writer buzzing about this
gripping play.' *Scotsman*

The Architect
'The whole play vibrates with such ambition and intelligence
– and in some places with such a breathtaking quality of
emotional courage and openness . . . David Greig is probably
the most gifted of the new Scottish playwrights of the
Nineties.' *Scotland on Sunday*

David Greig was born in Edinburgh. He is co-founder of
Suspect Culture with Graham Eatough which has produced
A Savage Reminiscence (Edinburgh Fringe, nominated for a
Guardian Student Drama Award), *And the Opera House
Remained Unbuilt, An Audience With Satan, The Garden, Stalinland*
(Edinburgh Fringe First winner), *Consider the Dish, Petra's
Explanation, Stations on the Border, One Way Street* (Traverse
Theatre, Edinburgh, and German tour) and *Airport*
(Tramway, Glasgow). Other plays include *Europe* (1994,
Traverse Theatre, Edinburgh; also Deutsches Theater, Berlin
and Staatsheater, Chemnitz) and *The Architect* (1996,
Traverse Theatre). His film debut, *Nightlife*, was premiered at
the Drambuie Edinburgh Film Festival in 1995 and
subsequently screened on BBC2. David is currently under
commission to the Royal National Theatre Studio and the
Traverse Theatre and has been awarded a Thames Television
Theatre Writers' bursary to work with the RSC.

David Greig

Europe
&
The Architect

B L O O M S B U R Y
LONDON • NEW DELHI • NEW YORK • SYDNEY

Bloomsbury Methuen Drama

An imprint of Bloomsbury Publishing Plc

50 Bedford Square	1385 Broadway
London	New York
WC1B 3DP	NY 10018
UK	USA

www.bloomsbury.com

Bloomsbury is a registered trade mark of Bloomsbury Publishing Plc

First published in Great Britain in 1996 by Methuen Drama

Europe first published in 1995 by Methuen Drama in *Frontline Intelligence 3*.
© David Greig, 1993
The Architect first published as a Methuen Drama Fast Track Playscript.
© David Greig, 1996

British Library Cataloguing-in-Publication Data
A catalogue record for this book is available from the British Library.

ISBN: PB: 978-0-4137-0880-9
ePDF: 978-1-4725-3832-1
ePUB: 978-1-4081-7628-3

Library of Congress Cataloging-in-Publication Data
A catalog record for this book is available from the Library of Congress.

Contents

Europe

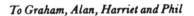
To Graham, Alan, Harriet and Phil

But where shall we go to today, my dear?
But where shall we go to today?

Auden, 'Refugee Blues'

Something unique is afoot in Europe, in what
is still called 'Europe' even if we no longer
know very well what or who goes by this name.

Derrida, *The Other Heading*

Europe was first performed at the Traverse Theatre, Edinburgh, on 21 October 1994. The cast was as follows:

Morocco	David Baker
Fret	Alasdair McCrone
Berlin	John Kazek
Adele	Louise Ironside
Katia	Sharon Maharaj
Sava	Finlay Walsh
Horse	Gregory Haiste
Billy	Michael Nardone

Chorus Played by members of the company

Directed by Philip Howard
Designed by Kenny MacLellan
Lighting by Michael Calf
Music by John Irvine

Characters

Morocco, *a local entrepreneur*
Fret, *the stationmaster*
Berlin, *a worker*
Adele, *the porter*
Katia, *a foreigner*
Sava, *a foreigner*
Horse, *a worker*
Billy, *a shop steward*

Setting: A small decaying provincial town in Europe. Autumn.

Act One

1 Morocco

Darkness . . .

An international express train passes the station. The train makes an incredible noise, building steadily as it approaches. Speed, metal and light dominate the theatre drowning everything for a moment in the train's elemental force. Slowly, as the sound dies, the lights come up.

Morocco *arrives in the town square. He is a dark man, unshaven and wearing a dusty suit and sunglasses. He has a heavy suitcase with him. In front of a blue neon sign for the calypso bar he lights a cigarette and puts his suitcase down and considers his situation.*

2 The First Chorus

1   Ours is a small town on the border, at various times on this side,

2   and,

3   at various times,

2   on the other,

1   but always

1, 2, 3   on the border.

4   We're famous for our soup,

5   for our factory which makes lightbulbs

1   and for being on the border.

6   On the plains at the heart of Europe

7   we're checkers of passports and clippers of tickets,

8   manufacturers of soup and light.

1   History has washed across us

2 Europe

2 in armies driving first west

3 then east

2 then west again.

4 Wave upon wave has crashed about us,

All but we've remained,

5 a rockpool on the shoreline,

6 inhabitants of the tidemark,

7 the place where driftwood is deposited,

8 beyond the cleansing reach of the waves.

1 Some places become used to the thud of industry.

2 Some places become used to the music of a cafe piano.

3 But here, in the interior,

4 we've become used to the stillness,

5 to the rhythm of the railway timetable

6 and the rustle of currency.

All We ask for very little here.

7 With things as they are we daren't ask for much.

8 Except that as you pass,

5 on your way to an older,

6 more beautiful

7 or more important place,

8 you remember that we are,

All in our own way,

1 also Europe.

Express train passing.

3 Arrivals

The town's station on an autumn morning. The station's architecture bears witness to the past century's methods of government. Hapsburg, Nazi and Stalinist forms have created a hybrid which has neither the romantic dusting of history, nor the gloss of modernity. The predominant mood is of a forgotten place. Timetables, out-of-date posters and sadly decrepit information signs hang from the walls. A plain wooden bench sits in the middle of the main hall. The floor is of dirty concrete and is unswept.

Fret *is in his office. We can't see him.*

In the corner of the waiting room is a blackboard with the chalked sign 'NO TRAINS' written in bold letters.

Adele *is on the station roof watching trains. A bundle of notebooks and brochures are arranged beside her. She hasn't seen* **Berlin** *arrive behind her.*

Sava, *a man in his late fifties, is sitting on the station bench, asleep huddled pathetically amongst belongings: a canvas bag, some polythene bags and an old suitcase. His clothes have not been changed for some weeks, perhaps months. They were not fashionable clothes to start with.*

Katia, *his daughter, sits next to him, straight-backed, awake.*

Fret   ADELE! ADELE, WHERE ARE YOU?

The train's noise subsides.

Fret (*emerging from the office carrying a bundle of timetables*)   Adele, I can't make head nor tail of these can you come and have a look please. (*Noticing* **Katia** *and* **Sava**.) . . . Oh.

Berlin Adele.

Fret Are you?

Adele   . . . It's you . . . (*Checking her watch.*) Ten past nine. (*She ticks it off in her notebook.*) Shouldn't you be at work?

Fret You're not? You're not?

Berlin   Fret said you'ld be here.

Fret   . . . Are you?

Adele   Isn't it beautiful? Look. Before it disappears.

Berlin   Yes. Adele. I.

Fret   Obviously not.

Fret, *believing they must be there for a reason, tries to ignore their presence.*

Berlin   Adele, I . . .

Fret   I need you to have a look at these timetables.

Adele   There, follow my hand . . . there! Where the track curves before the bridge . . . past the checkpoint . . . there! (*She points.*)

Fret   Now! Please!

Adele   Can you see it?

Berlin   I can see it. Look, Adele, I've been . . .

Fret   You're not waiting for a train or anything, are you?

Adele   It's going to Warsaw. Imagine . . . Warsaw.

Fret   Only you do realise there aren't any.

Fret *lays the timetables on the floor and attempts to study them.*

Berlin   I . . . had a surprise today.

Fret   Trains, I mean.
None.
They're all cancelled.

Berlin   A shock, in fact. I had a shock.

Fret   For today, at least.

Adele   I've never been to Warsaw.

Fret   None stopping.

Berlin   There was an announcement in the canteen.

Adele   I've unloaded parcels from Warsaw. I've sold tickets to Warsaw. I've seen Warsaw in pictures, but I've never been.

Berlin   Over breakfast . . . in the canteen.

Adele   Never actually.

Berlin   Billy told us two hundred jobs were going.

Fret   You realise there's no point in . . .?

Berlin   Over breakfast, he said there wasn't enough work. 'I'm sorry about that, lads.' He said,

Fret   It . . . pains me . . . to say it.

Berlin   'Sorry, lads.' . . . Like he was saying there wasn't enough ham.

Fret   A station is a place for trains, after all.

Berlin   Not enough work for us all to have some. That's the bottom line. He said.

Fret   It's a fair mistake to make . . . but there is a sign. (*He points. They ignore him. He returns to his office.*)

Berlin   Something's got to give.
He said a consultant had been.
Someone from head office.

Fret   I'm sorry for any inconvenience.

Berlin   The consultant said we've been living in a dreamland. Four men employed to run the furnace.

Fret   ADELE, THIS DOESN'T MAKE ANY SENSE!

Berlin   'Four men. Dreamland! Cloudcuckooland, crazy' . . . he said.

Fret   Of course it's all down to the changes.

Berlin   'You people can't be serious,' he said.

Fret   I'm sure you're aware of them.

Berlin   'I don't believe it,' he said.

Fret   The changes.

Berlin   He rolled his finger at the side of his head.
'Unbelievable.'

Fret   They're getting in everywhere.

Berlin   'Economic lunacy. Economic madness. Looks like someone's been telling you people bedtime stories.'

Fret   Like dirt.

Berlin   Someone's been telling me bedtime stories, Adele.

Fret   Muck.

Berlin   I've been sacked. Put out. Horse as well. All of us. Finished.

Fret   Waste of my time.

Berlin   What do you make of that?

Fret   Waste of your time. A great big waste.

Fret *goes back into his office.*

Berlin   Machines can run a furnace apparently.
Apparently they don't need furnacemen.

Adele   Berlin . . .

Berlin   Apparently, I've been unnecessary for some time.

Adele   Berlin, maybe it means something . . .

Berlin   . . . not just unnecessary, Adele, but harmful as well.

Adele   Maybe it's fate . . . maybe it's God.

Berlin   It would be just like him.

Adele   It could be a sign . . .

Berlin   A sort of 'Piss off, Berlin, you're out' sign?

Adele   A green light.
A chance.
Do you remember we said before . . . when the border opened . . . we said, 'What's to stop us?'
Do you remember? What's to stop us?
A factory, a job, a station.

That's all . . . a pissy job . . . nothing . . . worthless.
Maybe it's a chance, Berlin. A new start.

Berlin   You're not helping, Adele.

Adele   But you're free. Don't you see? You've been
released.

Berlin   I didn't want to be released, Adele. I can't do
anything else. Working the furnace is my job. It's all I know.
There's nothing else. Nowhere else for me to go.

Adele   Look . . . see there . . . at the edge of the forest. You
can see the border. Just. There. You can make out the wire.

Berlin   You might as well admit I'm finished, Adele.

Adele   Nothing changes on either side of it, the landscape
stays the same, there's just the wire. Hardly visible. Like a
thought.

Berlin   Listen to me! Listen to what I'm telling you.

Adele   It's as if the border's hardly there, as if you could
imagine it away. What do you think? As if you could just
walk through it . . . just cross the line.

Berlin   You don't make any sense, Adele. You've no idea.
I'm fucked. You're fucked. We're Fucked. Fucking out of it.
Out of the fucking running. Fucked utterly.

. . .

. . .

. . .

I'm sorry.

Fret *emerges holding the fat pile of timetables in his hand, defeated.*

Fret   Adele!

Berlin   I said sorry.

Fret   ADELE!

. . .

See this? Four hundred pages and none of it makes sense.
Times, stations, trains . . . They've no relation to anything.
Meaningless . . . they might just as well be foreign.

Berlin   I didn't mean . . .

Fret   Foreign books. ADELE! I can only think, things must have . . . somewhere along the line . . . In head office they must . . . I don't know . . . I don't follow . . . I just think THINGS MUST HAVE COME TO SOMETHING IF THE STATIONMASTER CAN'T FOLLOW THE TIMETABLE.

Berlin   I'm sorry. We need a chance to talk . . .

Adele   I've got to go.

Berlin   Adele. Adele.

Adele *doesn't reply. She leaves.* **Berlin** *is left standing alone.*

Express train passing.

4   A breach of regulations

Katia *and* **Sava** *as before.* **Katia** *is sitting and* **Sava** *is asleep in her lap. During the scene* **Sava** *wakes up. They might exchange a few words in low voices but they don't say much.*

Adele *and* **Fret** *are pinning up the new timetables around the station.*

Fret *disappears in and out of the office during the scene fetching drawing pins, timetable sheets etc.*

Adele   She looks foreign.

Fret *coming out of office.*

Fret   They've been here since this morning.

Adele   You did say there were no trains?

Fret   They ignored me. Just sat. Didn't even look at me.

Adele   Maybe they're on business. Between meetings.

Fret   Vagrants.

Fret *in office.*

Adele   Perhaps they're tourists . . .

Fret Here?

Adele They might be . . . Or she could be a journalist . . . on the trail of a hot story . . .

Fret Local Station In 'We waited for train but it never arrived' Drama.

Adele You never know. Maybe . . . or . . . maybe they're travelling incognito. On the run . . . spies, criminals, gun runners from Libya. Maybe they're supplying freedom fighters or terrorist factions in . . . England . . . with plastic explosives and mortars . . . maybe she's wanted by Interpol . . . maybe she's responsible for hundreds of deaths in dozens of cities . . .

Fret *out of office.*

Fret I don't care who they are they can't loiter on my platform . . . we're not a bloody youth hostel.

Adele I don't see what harm they're doing.

Fret It's my station.

Adele I don't see why they shouldn't wait . . . if they want to.

Fret It's a breach of regulations.

Adele Is it?

Fret Probably . . . I don't know . . . I'm not sure but it can't be allowed to continue . . .

Adele Why not?

Fret Because . . . because . . . Look, Adele, I don't mean to lecture you . . .

Adele But . . .

Fret *in office.*

Fret If you want to run a station like this you have to learn you can't just let things ride. Not in this job. You have to take control, get a hold of the reins early on . . . see what's happening and respond effectively with action . . .

Adele   I think he looks ill. Maybe he's ill? Maybe he can't
move. *She looks concerned.*

Fret *out of office.*

Fret   When you're in the railways, Adele, you're connected
to the heart of things . . . so you have to keep a constant
watch on every little situation because there's always the
possibility of repercussions along the line . . .

Adele *finally catches* **Katia's** *eye. They exchange a look.*

Fret *in office.*

Fret   A little delay in Levski North because the driver
wants a sardine sandwich or a garlic sausage from the kiosk.
Are you listening? This is your training, Adele . . . maybe the
driver was at school with the kiosk man, maybe a mutual
friend's getting married so they have a gossip . . . it's possible
. . . it's the sort of situation a stationmaster comes across
every day . . .

Adele   There's something . . . how would you describe it?
Something . . .

Fret   In that sausage, Adele, are the seeds of catastrophe
. . . because the next thing is the Cracow express is kept
waiting at the points . . .

Adele   . . . sophisticated, she looks . . . she's not from here
anyway . . . not local . . .

Fret   Ten minutes maybe it waits . . . so it's late in Cracow
where it has to connect with the Paris train. An entire
transcontinental train kept waiting for ten, maybe by this
stage, fifteen minutes . . .

Adele   She doesn't look like she'd be local anywhere . . .

Sava *produces a stove from their luggage and a small bottle of water.
He proceeds to light the stove to heat up the water for coffee.*

Fret   So appointments aren't kept, businessmen apologise;

Adele   No fixed abode, a traveller.

Fret Wives worry, husbands suspect, lovers are cheated of a few moments together, a gentle shudder across the skin of the nation . . . because the driver of the Levski train wants a garlic sausage . . . you let things slide on the railways and there are repercussions . . . that's one of the few things in this life you can be sure of. You can't just let things ride.

In front of them a small stove of water is boiling. **Adele** *is watching.* **Fret** *comes out . . .*

Fret   . . . (*Horrified.*)
They're cooking.
. . .
They're cooking.
. . .
They thought they'd just . . . have a cook.
On my platform.

THIS IS NOT A GYPSY ENCAMPMENT.

Determined, **Fret**, *returns to his office. After a moment, the tannoy plays a short irritating tune.*

Tune.

Fret (*coughs*)   Attention please, ladies and gentlemen, attention please . . . this is a passenger announcement. There will be no trains today. Trains today have been cancelled. The next train for passengers at this station will not be for some time . . . a long time . . . until further notice . . . (*He coughs.*) . . . we apologise for any inconvenience. This has been a passenger announcement on behalf of state railways. Thank you for your attention.

The tannoy plays a short irritating tune.

Fret *pops his head out of the office . . .* **Katia** *and* **Sava** *have taken no notice. Frustrated,* **Fret** *returns to the tannoy.*

Short irritating tune. **Katia** *notices the tune with annoyance.*

Adele He's right . . .

Fret The delay is due to . . . to . . .

Adele (*to* **Katia**)   The place is falling apart.

Fret   Re-structuring . . . restructuring which is . . .

Adele   It's upsetting . . . he's upset . . . as you can see.

Fret   It's necessary . . . necessary restructuring is taking place . . . for your benefit . . .

Adele   The system's collapsing . . .

Fret   And so there aren't any trains . . . Passengers are therefore advised to make alternative arrangements . . .

Fret pops his head out . . . seeing they have taken no notice . . . he returns to the tannoy in fury.

Sava *is about to reply tentatively to* **Adele**'s *question when he is drowned by . . .*

. . . a short irritating tune.

Fret   . . . Attention . . . Achtung . . . it's obviously stupid to wait for a train when a train is obviously not coming.

. . .

. . .

Please go now.

He comes out of his office.

All right. Show me your tickets.

Adele   Fret!

Katia   We don't have any tickets.

Fret   How do you expect to get on a train without proper tickets?

Katia   We expect nothing.

Adele   He gets this way . . . he's a stickler . . .

Fret   You expect nothing?

Katia   Nothing.

Fret   I see.

Sava   We're making tea. Would you like some?

Fret   You do realise you're flying in the face of all reason?
. . .
You're not bloody inter-railers are you?

Sava   You wouldn't have a teaspoon of sugar at all?

Adele   I'll get it . . .

Fret   Stay there! Inter-railers — travelling about without a bloody destination . . . expecting nothing . . . letting it happen . . . getting on and off trains with complete disregard for the principle of the thing.

Katia   Be careful of the stove.

Fret   Sleeping in stations . . . in stations, for God's sake. International Casanovas and their Australian girlfriends. 'Let it happen' they say . . . as though getting on a train was like getting old, or getting sick or dying or something. Well it's not, not in my station at any rate. In my station you buy a ticket, you get on a train and you go where you say you're going to go. Expect nothing. Bloody hell.

Sava   You'll hurt your foot . . . boiling water will fall on your foot.

Fret   Expect nothing! . . . It's a passenger's job to expect something, it's a civic responsibility . . . when you stop expecting anything from people you're only a step away from anarchism. Give me your pass, show me your pass!

Katia   We don't have any pass.

Fret   No pass. I see. Anarchists.

Katia   This is a waiting room . . . we're waiting. We don't need a pass.

Adele   She's right.

Fret   All right, come on, party's over . . . this rubbish . . . all finished now . . . (*He starts to pick up their belongings and stuff them carelessly into their bags.*)

Sava   Watch the tea for goodness sake!

Adele   Fret!

The stove is knocked over. The water spills.

Sava   Oh dear.

Fret   (*a cry of pain, boiling water has poured onto his foot*).

Adele (*to* **Katia**)   I'm sorry.

Katia   I told you.

Fret   TYPICAL . . . THAT'S FUCKING TYPICAL . . .

Katia (*to* **Sava**)   I told you this would happen.

Fret   Indicative . . . that's what you are. Indicative of the whole fucking situation.

Adele   I'll get the mop.

Fret   The whole thing! (*A cry of pain.*) . . . The whole bloody thing's fucked.

Fret *sits down disconsolately nursing his foot. No one moves.*

Adele   Should I get a bandage?

Fret   Do whatever . . . just whatever . . . I don't care . . . let it happen . . .

Sava   Excuse me. We've come a long way. . . .

Katia   We won't disturb you. We intend to be gone soon.

Sava   All we want is to spend a short while here in peace. We're not planning a coup . . . we're not bandits . . .

Katia   I can assure you, we dislike it here as much as you do.

Sava   I'm sorry if things are bad for you just now but things are bad where we come from as well. We've been blown around from place to place for a long time and this is where we've come to rest. For now. The fault is neither yours nor ours but belongs to the random chaotic winds of current events. I suggest you calm down and we'll have a look at your timetables if that's the problem . . . I've worked on the railways myself. I know the system. If there aren't any trains then we'll be in nobody's way . . .

Katia   We're good at staying hidden. We're practiced.

Sava   Maybe we can even be of some use.

Katia   Someone to blame if nothing else.

Sava *awaits some response.* **Fret** *has no response to give. Pause. Noise of train builds up. Express train passes.*

5   Flying boat people

Inside the Calypso Bar in the afternoon. The Calypso Bar is shabby and has counters and formica tables. The chairs are hard like school chairs. **Berlin**, **Billy** *and* **Horse** *are nursing beers.*

Berlin   A video.

Horse   A datsun.

Billy   Dirty books.

Berlin   Beer.

Horse   A trip to the mountains.

Berlin   To the beach.

Billy   To the sunny Med.

Horse   To be naked on the sand.

Berlin   To go brown in the heat.

Horse   Like a pig on a spit.

Billy   Surrounded by women.

Berlin   Slaves.

Billy   An endless supply of ice cold beer.

Horse   A magical cock. A magical cock that can piss ice cold beer.

. . .

A change of mood.

Billy   Seriously, I might build a house, maybe . . .

Berlin   A cabin in the forest.

Horse   A bachelor pad.

Berlin   With your own hands . . .

Billy   Miles from anywhere.

Horse   Only the wolves for company.

Berlin   Hunt your own food . . .

Billy   Self reliance.

Horse   You could live . . .

Berlin   Until you died . . .

Billy   In the middle of the forest.

Horse   No one'd ever know.

. . .

A change of mood.

Berlin   When you think . . . When you think what . . . Fuck, I want to . . .

Horse   Give someone a doing. . . .

Billy   A kicking.

Berlin   Some fuck.

Horse   That fucking consultant.

Billy   And the other cunts.

Berlin   All the fuckers.

Horse   Pan their cunts in.

Billy   Cunting pan them.

Berlin   Waste them, Billy. I want to waste them.

All   Fuckin waste the cunts.

. . .

Billy   Seriously but. What'll you do?

Berlin   Waste them. Like I said.

Horse   Who?

Berlin   Them, someone.

Billy   You wouldn't though, would you? Not really.

Horse   Why not?

Billy   Because it would be stupid.

Berlin   Would it?

Billy   Aye it would.

Berlin   Is that so?

Billy   It is.

Berlin   That's what you say is it?

Billy   Aye.

Berlin   Stupid?

Billy   Berlin.

Berlin   That's me. That's my name. So what?

A slight pause.

Horse   I think it could be good.

Berlin   What?

Horse   What you said.

Berlin   When?

Horse   Just then. What you were saying. I'm with you.

Berlin   Good.

Billy   Fine.

Berlin   Right.

. . .

A change of mood.

Horse   Did you ever see that video? The one where the bloke . . .

Berlin   The one where he goes mental . . .

Horse   Shoots everyone in the train . . .

Billy   Never seen it. . . .

Horse   You'ld need to get a gun . . .

Billy   What happens to him in the end?

Horse   Blaze of bullets . . .

Berlin   Flesh flies . . .

Billy   Fantastic.

Horse   Brilliant. Work of a brilliant mind.

Berlin   Blood splatters all over the joint . . .

Horse   Classic of the genre.

Billy   Look at those pricks.

Horse   Where?

Billy   There. The wee cunts.

Horse   The skinheads.

Billy   Aye.

Horse   What about them?

Billy   Well . . . You didn't used to see that.

Berlin   They look under age.

Billy   Not here. You didn't used to get that in here.

Berlin   You ought to tell their dads.

Horse   Twats.

Billy   It's coming to something.

Berlin   Coming to something all right . . .

Horse   It's not right.

Billy   You're right.

Berlin   It's all wrong.

. . .

Horse   What would you do, Berlin, if you were . . . ?

Berlin   What?

Horse   In charge.

Billy   Of what?

Horse   You know . . .

Billy   President?

Horse   King.

Berlin   Dictator.

Horse   All of that.

Berlin   I'd . . . I'd sort it out . . .

Billy   How?

Berlin   I'd do the business.

Billy   You would have to face economical realities.

Horse   Harsh ones.

Billy   Stiff ones.

Horse   The cold winds of recession.

Billy   Too many workers not enough jobs.

Berlin   Yeah, well. I'm not, am I. I'm not president.

Horse   But if you were.

Berlin   I'd . . . fuck Jackie Kennedy . . . and Marilyn Monroe, I'd buy expensive women for myself and my friends, smart suit, smart car, smart life . . . smart.

Horse   I'd get rid of the blacks.

Berlin   Which ones?

Horse   All of them . . . boat people.

Billy   Boat People?

Horse   Steal our jobs.

Berlin   Boat People?

Horse   Apparently.

Billy   But . . .

Berlin   We're miles from the sea.

Horse   They fly them.

Billy   Flying boat people.

Horse   Apparently.

Berlin   Where did you learn that?

Horse   A bloke told me.

Billy   You should be over there . . . with Go Balls and his mates.

Horse   Maybe I should.

Berlin   You'ld suit a skinhead.

Billy   You'ld really do it . . . if you were dictator . . .

Horse   First I'd give all the blacks' jobs back to us.

Billy   And then what?

Horse   Then I'd . . .

Billy   What?

Horse   Well, I'd . . .

Billy   What?

Horse   . . . fuck Jackie Kennedy . . .

Billy   And then . . .?

Horse   I'd . . . Retire. Give it all up. Live in a hut in forest. What about you?

Billy   I've decided already.

Berlin   What?

Billy   I'm leaving.

Horse   It's early.

Billy   Leaving here. Leaving town. Vamoose. Skidaddle.

Horse   But . . . Billy . . . Billy Bilbo . . .

Billy   Saddle up and ride my pony . . .

Horse   Old Bill . . .

Billy   Get out while the gettings good . . . I say.

Horse   My old mate Billington . . .

Berlin   Are you serious?

Billy   Couldn't be more so.

Horse   Bilboglio . . . mate . . . pal . . .

Berlin   Why?

Billy   Look around you, Berlin.
The place is fucked.
We live in a dirty, nothing place . . . it's fucked, mate.
On its way down. Sinking. Anyone can see that. You just
need to look around you . . .

Horse   The skins?

Billy   The town's sick, fading fast, last legs time . . .

Berlin   They're just wee boys, Billy . . .

Horse   They're just . . .

Billy   Wolves looking for scraps . . . flies on shit. I'm
getting out.

Berlin   But this is . . . where you live, Billy.

Billy   I don't live here, it's a weight, a stone in the stomach,
it's not a place to live it's a place to die.

Horse   I like it.

Billy   You keep it.

Horse   Well, I never thought . . .

Berlin   Never saw you as the leaving type, Billy.

Billy   We should all leave. Get out . . . split up . . . look
around.

Horse   But . . . what about . . . solidarity . . .?

Berlin   We always said we'd stick together.

Billy   Losers stick together . . . crowds . . . sheep . . . that's sticking together . . . not me. No way. . . . I'm on my own. I've jumped ship. I'll try my luck with the sharks. Strike out . . . swim for the horizon while my head's above water . . .

. . .

Horse   Cabin in the woods for me. Fend for myself.

Berlin   I'm staying here. Staying put. Do what I can to keep sane. It's home, isn't it? Roots. I've got a wife.

Billy   Get out while you can, if you can.

Berlin   I can leave any time if I want to . . .

Billy   Bullshit, you're trapped.

Berlin   I just don't want to leave at this moment in time.

Billy   You're trapped.

Berlin   Fuck you I am.

Billy   You're stuck, under the bedclothes, can't get up and face the day in case the world's moved on in the night. Keep the curtains closed and lie still . . . stuck. That's you.

Berlin   Fuck you, Billy . . . I just want . . .

Horse   . . . a magical cock that can piss cold beer.

Berlin   And a magical arse that can shit cash.

A change of mood.

Express train passes.

6   A quiet talk

At night. **Katia** *and* **Sava** *are amongst their shabby suitcases and bags.* **Sava** *has a blanket around his shoulders.* **Katia** *is obviously cold, she is smoking.*

Sava   Sit down. We can share the blanket.

Katia   I'm all right.

Sava You'll freeze.

Katia I'm all right.

Sava What're you thinking about?

Katia Nothing.

Sava You're chewing your lip.

Katia Am I?

Sava When you were eight and used to take your mother's hand for the walk to school, you chewed your lip like that.

Katia We shouldn't have stopped. We were safer travelling. Keeping moving.

Sava You chewed your lip and frowned. While your mother smiled and passed the time with other mothers you stood at her knee and frowned like you disapproved.

Katia I think we've made a mistake. That's all.

Sava You held her hand and tried to pull her along the road. When the other children were kicking stones you were buttoned up, in smart shoes and your eyes fixed straight ahead. No deviations, no detours.

Katia We'll end up stuck here. At least while we were hidden we were flexible. We had the chance to move on.

Sava Taking responsibility for everything. Making sure.

Katia Now we're out in the open.

Sava Sit down. Come on. Sit next to your dad. Give your old man a hug.

Katia I'm not cold.

Sava Of course you're cold. Come here.

Katia It's fine, Dad. Look. I said I was fine.

Sava What's the matter . . . I smell . . . is that the problem?

Katia Dad.

Sava   You don't smell so great yourself . . . We've sweated away the summer in dirty camps. The bus was an oven. An overcrowded oven. We're bound to smell a bit . . . come on . . . sit. Stop worrying. We'll be all right.

Katia   I've made a plan.

Sava   Another one.

Katia   There won't be any trains here, the stationmaster said so himself. It's pointless staying. So we'll have to hitch. If you stand back from the road and I get cleaned up a bit we'll get lifts easily, if not we'll keep walking. In a bigger place we can get lost. We can find papers, passports, contacts . . . something. First we need to get out of here. Berlin maybe . . . Paris . . . Milan. Somewhere big, I'm not sure yet. I just know we can't stay here. It's too small. We're too visible.

Sava   I'm tired of plans, Katia.

Katia   I'll get a job in a club or a bar. We'll get a room.

Sava   You don't want to work in a club . . . you've been to college . . . you belong in an office . . . somewhere clean, somewhere modern.

Katia   A bar . . . something . . . whatever . . . then we can start . . . a room, some money . . .

Sava   A bar . . . it's so undignified.

Katia   A room and some money first and I'll worry about dignity later.

Sava   You plan too much. Tomorrow's tomorrow . . . tonight it's late, we've come a long way, try to sleep.

Katia   I've got things to work out.

Sava   You'll make yourself ill.

Katia   I'm trying to be realistic. I'm trying to assess the options. We can't stay here.

Sava   A station's as good a place as any. I like stations. They make me feel at home.

Katia   We'll get sent back, they'll leave us to rot in some transit camp over the border.

Sava   Maybe. I don't think so.

Katia   I've seen it happen.

Sava   You underestimate people.

Katia   Believe me, they invented hate in places like this. There's not much other nightlife. I've seen it before. I saw it at home.

Sava   You underestimate human nature. It's human nature to be suspicious at first. But you forget that it's also human nature to see the truth of a situation when the situation's made clear. That's what you forget. We're dignified people. We're decent people. These things are valued everywhere.

Katia   You still don't see it, do you?

Sava   I don't see it the way you do.
. . .
Katia, we're not in some savage country on the other side of the world. Look around you, look at the architecture. Listen to the sounds from the street. You can smell the forest. We're a long way from home but we're still in Europe. We'll be looked after. Our situation will be understood.

Katia   Europe. Snipers on the rooftops, mortars in the suburbs and you said: 'This is Europe . . . we must stay in Europe.' So we stayed, even after the food ran out: 'This is Europe.' When the hospitals were left with nothing but alcohol and dirty bandages . . . I warned you and you still said: 'This is Europe . . . honesty will prevail, sense will win . . . this war is an aberration . . . a tear in the fabric. In time it'll be sewn up again and things will look as good as new.'

Sava   What are you saying?

Katia   I'm saying I believed you.

Sava It was the truth. It still is the truth. Katia, the important thing is that we never give in to animalism, to barbarism.

Katia At least animals protect their own.

Sava So. This is what you wanted to talk about.

Katia Maybe.

Sava Say it then.

Katia We stayed and . . . We stayed.

Sava Go on.

Katia It doesn't matter.

Sava Say what you mean to say.

Katia Forget it. I just think we should move on.

Sava Is that everything?

Katia Yes.

Sava That's all you want to say.

Katia For now.

Sava Then it's late. We'll talk about it in the morning.

Katia Sure.

Sava Come and share the blanket.

Katia I'm all right.

Express train passing.

7   Look what Berlin found on the steps

Inside the Calypso Bar. **Horse** *and* **Billy** *are drinking.* **Berlin** *enters with* **Morocco**. **Morocco** *is uneasy.*

Berlin Horse, Billy, look what I found . . .

Horse Morocco!

Billy I don't believe it.

Berlin   On the steps of the hotel . . .

Morocco   The hotel . . .

Berlin   Dark suit, smart, dark glasses, really smart . . .

Morocco   I do what I can . . .

Billy   Long time no see, Morocco.

Morocco   Too long.

Berlin   What did I say when I saw you? What did I say . . .

Morocco   . . .

Berlin   I said . . . fuck me. I said fuck me.

Morocco   He did. He said that.

Berlin   I said it because I love this man. I love him. I've
loved him since we were both so high and he used to sell me
dirty pictures he'd stolen from you boys . . .

Morocco   No.

Billy   So that's where they went.

Berlin   If you can't rip off your friends, who can you rip off.

Horse   Morocco the porno dealer!

Morocco   I didn't do it . . . he's making it up for effect.

Berlin   Our local entrepreneur.

Billy   I'm surprised you came back. I thought you were
gone for good.

Morocco   I missed the old place. I missed it. Honest to God
I swear. I missed you boys. I missed the bar . . . I've been all
over the continent from the Baltic to Gibraltar but even an
entrepreneur has feelings . . . I missed it . . .

Berlin   I don't believe you. The only thing you worry
about missing is the chance to buy dollars.

Morocco   I pined. I swear. That's the only word for it.
Pined. Worse than any dog. Alone in the train from Vienna
to Belgrade I passed the time with dreams of home . . . I
knew I had to come back in the end.

Horse   What are you selling this time, Morocco?

Morocco   Selling? Nothing. Nothing . . . not today . . .
today I've come with nothing except presents . . . see . . .

He opens his suitcase.

Vodka.

Horse   Jesus.

Morocco   One each . . . see . . . friends. (*He gives them each a
bottle.*) Now . . . a toast . . . to the boys. I heard the bad news.
The factory etc. I heard . . . I'm sorry. Believe me. Still, one
door closed another opens. It's from Poland this. Best there
is. To home . . . where we all belong.

Billy   It doesn't belong to me . . . Morocco.

Morocco   Of course it belongs to you. Who else can it
belong to? It belongs to me. It belongs to everyone . . . to us.

Billy   You've got money, Morocco, you wouldn't
understand.

Morocco   Take it from me. It's the same old place. I may
have been away, but I see the old faces, smell the old smells.
When you're a business traveller like me, Horse, you carry
your memories everywhere with you like precious stones and
every night, in hotels, on trains, in ditches, you take them out
and count them, you examine every facet, you count and
recount for comfort's sake till you fall asleep. Believe me your
memories are more valulable than money, never mind the
currency.

Horse   Is this stuff nicked?

Morocco   Never.

Berlin   Looks dodgy to me. Smuggled over the border?

Morocco   No. It's just . . . export . . . import export.

Horse   Import export? You're a fucking smuggler.

Morocco   No . . . What else is a border for?

Horse   We could get you arrested, Morocco.

Morocco *draws a line down the middle of the table. He uses the bottles and glasses etc. to demonstrate his theories.*

Morocco   This is what a border is. See . . .?

Berlin   What?

Morocco   A magic money line. See. You pass something across it and it's suddenly worth more. Pass it across again and now it's cheaper. More . . . less . . . less . . . more . . . fags, drink, jobs, cars . . . less is more, more or less . . . see . . . magic money just for crossing a magic line. I'm not a smuggler, I'm a magician, an illusionist. There's no crime in that.

Berlin   The money's real enough though, isn't it. Mr Smart Shoes. You've done well.

Again **Morocco** *demonstrates, this time he performs the trick.*

Morocco   I swear to God it's a conjuring trick. Swear to God. Give me a dollar . . . abracadabra . . . I give you roubles back . . . give me some roubles . . . come on . . . give . . . hey presto . . . Deutchmarks. It's all imaginary . . . none of it's real, none. You just have to think up the trick . . . it's easy . . .

Billy   Maybe to you. But there has to be . . .

Horse   A catch.

Berlin   There has to be rules.

Morocco   The more rules the better. The more rules there are the more people get caught in the net and the more it takes magicians to find the gaps. I need rules. I feed on them.

Billy   You're a trader by your nature, Morocco.

Berlin   A slippery customer . . .

Billy   You were born to it . . . We're just workers.

Horse   We just make stuff . . .

Berlin   It's all we can do.

Morocco   Then you're fucked. Anyone can make. Anyone. Koreans, Japs . . . English, anyone . . . they make. The magic comes in the buying and selling. You move something from place to place and money sticks to it . . . like a sticky sweet picks up fluff. Take it from me. I swear to God it's magic.

Horse   Any cunt . . .

Berlin   Any one.

Morocco   You know what I mean. I'm only telling you the truth.

Berlin   We got the gist, Morocco.

Horse   Followed the thread.

Morocco   . . . come on . . . have another one . . . have another I've got plenty . . .

Morocco *shares out more vodka.*

Horse   So Morocco's a . . . travelling magician . . .

Morocco   At your service. Whatever you desire . . .

Horse   Can you magic me a cock that'll piss cold beer.

Berlin   Or an arse that shits cash.

Express train passing.

8   Trainspotting

Adele *at dawn, unlocking the station doors.* **Katia** *and* **Sava** *are asleep.* **Katia** *is sitting slightly apart asleep.* **Adele** *kneels beside here, at a slight distance and looks at her. Some moments pass.*

Katia   What? What's going . . . oh . . . it's you . . . look . . . we'll be out in a minute.

Adele   I didn't think you'ld be awake . . . it's early.

Katia   . . . we'll be gone in a minute . . . we'll go.

Adele   You can go back to sleep . . . it's not important . . . the first train's passing . . . in five minutes . . . I've come to . . .

Katia   To what?

Adele   To watch.

Katia   To watch what?

Adele   I'm sorry?

Katia   What happens at five thirty in the morning?

Adele   A train passes. Vienna. I watch them from the roof.

Katia   You're trainspotting?

. . .

Adele   Have you ever been to Vienna?

Katia   No.

Adele   Budapest?

Katia   Once.

Adele   You've been!

Katia   Once. Why?

Adele   It's where the train goes. (*Consulting brochures.*) Hungary's ancient capital.

Katia   Yes.

Adele   City of contrasts.

Katia   I suppose.

Adele   Beautiful Hapsburg Buda nestling in the hills.

Katia   I don't remember.

Adele   And the glories of bustling Pest.

Katia   Yes.

Adele   What was it like?

Katia   It was nice . . .

Adele   Nice . . .

Katia   Look, we needed a place to stay . . .

Adele   A big hotel on the banks of the Danube.

Katia   What?

Adele   Is that where you stayed?

Katia   I mean here . . . that's why we're still here, this morning. I'm sorry if it's a problem. We stayed the night. We slept here.

Adele   Tell me more.

Katia   It was cold . . . it's a station, I suppose, not a hotel. You can't be blamed for the temperature.

Adele   Tell me more about Budapest.

Katia   It was a long time ago. I don't remember.

Adele   Was it different?

Katia   To what?

Adele   To . . . this.

Katia   Slightly. Are you going to throw us out or not?

Adele   I've read about it, imagined it, I've been there so often in my head. I think I'd recognise it. I think I'd remember it. Maybe we could go back together.

Katia   I don't know what you're talking about.

Sava   Hmmm?

Adele   Five thirty-two . . . nearly time.

Sava   What's . . . going . . .

Katia   Shhh

They freeze.

Sava   Katia . . . is that . . . I thought . . .

Katia   It's nothing, Dad . . . you're dreaming.

Sava   Hmm . . .

There's a pause.

Adele   He's your father?

Katia   He's tired. We've been travelling. I'll wake him up if you want us to leave . . . otherwise he needs some sleep . . .

Adele   Is your husband . . .? Are you . . .?

Katia   I'm not married.

Adele   But you're . . . I mean . . .

Katia   Nice looking girl like me? I know. Look, I'd like to chat but . . .

Adele   I didn't . . . mean . . . I meant. It's unusual. Isn't it? Not to be married.

Katia   Is it? Look, do you want something?

Adele   No.

Katia   You're very inquisitive.

Adele   Just a conversation . . .?

Katia   I don't do conversation.

Adele   I only . . . I . . .

Katia   You're . . . what? What do you want?

Adele   . . . it's not that . . . it's just . . .

Katia   It's too early to work? You're not after throwing us out. So what do you want?

Adele   It's nothing special . . . I like to sit . . .
I like to watch the trains in the mornings, that's all.
. . .

Katia   Lovely.

Adele   The view, the forest, you can see across the town . . . that's all.

Katia   You do this every morning?

Adele   Most.

Katia   When there's a train due?

Adele   You can see it coming for miles . . . out of the hills, across the fields into the forest . . . When it comes through the station you can almost touch it.

Katia   An early morning epiphany would you say?

Adele   I don't know. I . . . Would you?

Katia   . . .?

Adele   You wouldn't . . .?

Katia   I wouldn't what?

Adele   Like to . . .

Katia   . . .?

Adele   Just if you wanted.

Katia   What?

Adele   . . . come with me.

Katia   You're not going to throw us out?

Adele   No. Of course not . . . Please.

Katia   I don't know what to make of you.

Adele   Don't make anything.

Katia   Very intriguing. You're not psychotic, are you?

Adele   I . . .

Katia   Only whenever I meet intriguing women they always turn out to be crazed in some way.

Adele   I'm not what you think.

Katia   That's what they all say.

Adele (*looks at watch*)   It's nearly time.

She climbs up to the roof.

It's coming. Hurry up.

Katia *follows her*.

Katia   Is this it?

Adele   There.

Katia   I can't see anything.

Adele   It's miles away still. Watch! It'll disappear in a minute . . . the lights get lost in the forest.

Katia *sits. It's still cold. She holds her body to keep warm.*

Katia   Christ, it's freezing out here.

Adele   It's come from Amsterdam.

Katia   I'll probably get piles.

Adele *grabs her hand and points it in the direction of the train.*

Adele   Look. Follow my hand. A chain of lights, look for a little chain of lights . . . a chain of Amsterdam diamonds . . .

A pause. She lets go of **Katia**'s *hand and moves away slightly.*

Fret *unlocks the station door. Loudly.* **Sava** *is asleep under the blanket. He wakes up. They look at each other.*

Fret   . . .

Sava   . . .

Fret   You're on the floor.

Adele *is staring at* **Katia**.

Katia   Please don't gaze at me.

Adele   Sorry.

Sava   Sorry . . . we eh . . . stayed . . .

Fret   I'll have to sweep it now. My floor.

Sava   Yes.

Fret   That one.

Sava *looks about him.*

Fret   . . . the one you're on.

Katia   You can look if you want. But I can't bear gazing.

Adele   Sorry.

Sava   I'll get up right away.

Fret   You will.

Sava   Just now.

Fret   Yes.

Sava (*groans*)   I can see my breath in front of me, it's so cosy under the blanket. I hate getting up in the winter, don't you?

Fret   I'm sorry?

Sava   I was just saying . . .

Fret   I don't think I wanted to banter. Did I look like I wanted to banter?

Sava   No.

Fret   Right.

Fret *goes into his office.* **Sava** *gets up quickly and bundles up his blanket.*

Katia   You're doing it again?

Adele   I wasn't, I was looking for the train.

Fret *emerges from his office with a brush. He holds it as though it was a weapon of defence.*

Sava   You know, you might be ill.

Fret   What?

Sava   You seem edgy. Upset, sarcasm, nerves. You look terrible. Perhaps you've got acid in the stomach. They're classic symptoms.

Fret   Perhaps I'm just nervous, sarcastic and upset. The symptoms are the same. It's hard to tell.

Katia   I'm not a tropical fish.

Sava *takes the brush.*

Sava   I'll give you a hand if you like.

Fret   Thank you.

Sava *begins to sweep.* **Fret** *inspects the timetables and tries to work out when the trains are due today. He is about to write them down on the blackboard.*

Adele   Where do you come from?

Katia   Does it matter?

Adele   I'm only asking.

Katia   I'm not sure.

Adele   Not sure?

Katia   Like I said. I'm not sure.

Adele   But. You must know. Everyone knows where they come from.

Katia   The place I came from isn't there any more. It disappeared.

Adele   A place can't just disappear.

Katia   Its name was taken off the maps and signposts. I couldn't find it anywhere.

Adele   . . . its name might have changed but the place must still be there. It's the same place . . . isn't it?

Katia   There's no way of checking.

Fret   You . . . you're waiting for a train, aren't you?

Sava   Well . . .

Fret (*he points to the timetables*)   These – rubbish. Meaningless rubbish.

Sava   Timetables are always difficult to follow.

Fret   You try. Go on, imagine you're a passenger.

Sava   I see.

Fret   OK. Imagine you want to travel from here to here overnight.

Sava   From where . . . here? . . . Right.

Fret   Now ordinarily you change trains here, in this station. Just after passport control at the border . . . then you'ld wait for one of the slow local trains in the morning.

Sava   I see. What do you want to know?

Fret   Imagine that's the journey. What would you do?

Adele   Maybe I can help. I've a map of Europe. What was it called, the town . . .?

Katia   It had a number of names. None of them stuck.

Adele   What did it look like? Big, small . . . what?

Katia   It looked like a small town. The sort of place people come from. Not the sort of place they go to, particularly.

Sava   Aha! A knife and fork. Does that mean I can use the buffet?

Fret   Restaurant car. Only for first-class ticket holders.

Sava   Oh. But overnight I'd want to eat.

Fret   You can pack banana sandwiches.

Sava   Well, I think I would take the international express to Sofia which goes through Wroclaw . . . change there . . . now there's a wait I think . . .

Adele   Perhaps . . . if you know what it looked like . . . that would be a clue.

Katia   I didn't recognise it the last time I saw it. Its appearance had changed considerably. It was difficult to tell if it was the same place. I had to ask a policeman.

Adele   What did he say?

Katia   He said he didn't know. He was from somewhere else. He was new to the place himself.

Adele   Didn't you recognise anything?

Katia   At midday the place was still. Everyone was indoors to escape the sun. I stood on the street kicking dust and listening to insects. The feeling of stillness. I recognised that. Apart from the stillness I could see nothing that I knew. Nothing familiar.

Adele   How had it changed?

Katia   It reminded me of a relative whose face has been torn off.

Adele   You think I'm ignorant. Don't you?

Sava   Now is it Friday?

Fret   It's not Friday.

Sava   So it's not a starred day and we've agreed I don't need a sleeper carriage. Let me see now . . .

Adele   . . . I know about where you're from. I know about the war. I know about all that. I read the papers. I asked a question from simple human curiosity. I want to know you. I want to know about you. I've not been very far in my life, I've not travelled, not like you. But I'm not ignorant. You don't have to humour me.

Adele *starts to go*.

Katia   What about your train?

Adele   It'll be there tomorrow.

Katia   Wait.
Please.
I'm sorry. I was being rude and defensive.
I can't help it. I said I wasn't good at conversation.
Please stay.

Adele   The war must have . . . affected you. I understand.

Katia   Oh no. I was rude and defensive before the war. The war just gave me a chance to practice.

Adele   Quiet!

Katia   What?

Adele   Listen.

Katia   What?

Adele   Listen. You're not listening. Stay still.

Katia   The train?

Adele   It's coming out of the forest. It's getting nearer.

Katia   What do we do now?

Adele   We wait.

Katia   You certainly know how to show a girl a good time, Adele.

Sava   I don't think it can be done, Mr Fret.

Fret   See! It makes no sense.

Sava   I think this station's closed.

Fret   Exactly. It's rubbish. Balls.

Sava   Here, you see. In small writing. This station's marked with an x.

Fret (*reading*)   'Station no longer in operation.'

Sava   I think you are, Mr Fret.

Fret   . . . what . . .

Sava   No Longer Operative as of . . . next month.

Fret   No. No.

Adele   I'm glad you came to watch. I didn't think. Someone like you . . . You're not bored, are you?

Katia   Bored, no.

Adele   Only I don't often meet foreigners. The trains are full of them, obviously, but they usually don't bother to get off. No one stops here. I just wanted to make friends.

Katia   Friends are like children, they're fine when they're other people's, but I wouldn't want any of my own.

Adele   Sometimes they just happen to you.

Sava   It says here you can take the bus from Lezno.

Fret   A bus! A bus! How can a grown man take the bus with any dignity. Sitting with students and chickens, yobs and failures.

Adele   Quarter to six, it's nearly time . . . any minute. Come on.

Sava   I understand how you must feel . . .

Fret   Do you?

Sava   I said before. I worked on the railways as well. I understand.

Adele   It creeps up on you. You'll feel it soon in your feet.

Fret   I don't understand it at all. It makes no sense to me.

Adele   And then your legs. You'll feel it come closer.

Fret   Since they opened the border the trains don't have to stop here any more.

Adele   You can feel the concrete shake.

Fret   It used to be we had a customs post here and pass control and everything. Now they do all that in between stops. The border doesn't mean much when you're on a train. So long as your pass is checked somewhere in between . . . it's more efficient.

Katia   I can hear it. I can hear it now.

Fret   I said to them. Don't expect me to stand in the way of change. I'm all for it. I'm a railwayman. I'm all for progress.

Adele   And now the horn . . . any second.

A train horn in the distance.

Fret   I'm all for going forward. Things have to get better. Machines get bigger, smoother . . . the engineering safer. I'm all for efficiency.

Adele   Thirty coaches long, the carriages at the front are from Holland, then some German, some from Poland. Tonnes and tonnes of steel . . . wood and glass . . .

The noise is building up.

Fret   So now they tell me this. Thirty years of progress, thirty years of laying down tracks and making trains and they send me this . . .

Sava   I understand.

Adele   . . . now the lights. See . . . you can see in at the people in the carriages . . . sitting, smoking, reading papers . . . ever since I was small I've stood up here to watch . . . a train full of everything. Every kind of thing from everywhere's inside it. Everything from everywhere is on that train and it's coming through here . . . stay still. (*She's shouting now.*) Hold still and feel it . . . can you feel it? Can you feel it . . .

The train's noise is at its peak. The train passes.

Act Two

9   The Second Chorus

1 & 2 are women.

1   Autumn's arrived in our town,

2   changing the colour of the forest,

3   bringing rain,

4   bringing wolves.

5   On the plains, at the heart of Europe,

6   we build fires,

7   strip fields,

8   and make soup.

1   But, late at night,

2   at the forest's end,

3   where the housing blocks sit in mud,

4   at the edge of the town,

5   wolves move among the bins,

6   dragging black sacks into the dark like killed deer.

7   Men stand at the bar counter and complain.

Men   We never got wolves before,

8   before they hid in the woods all winter,

3   now they sniff around the shadows at the bottom of the stairwell.

1   Smoke and the smell of beer hangs over the men.

2   Their voices creep out onto the dark street,

4   what's happened to this place?

5   I don't recognise it any more.

6   Maybe we lost it in a game of cards.

7   Maybe it disappeared into the forest.

8   Maybe it was stolen while our backs were turned.

All   Only it isn't our place any more.

1   Our place was taken in the night.

8   Our place slipped away while we were asleep.

10   Conversation

Adele *and* **Berlin**. *The television is on. Brochures lie around the floor.* **Adele** *has a pencil and paper and is writing down information.*

Berlin   Switch it off.

Adele   It's the holiday programme.

Berlin   I want to talk.

Adele   She's going to France this week and . . .

Berlin   I don't give a fuck.

Adele   To Marseilles.

Berlin   Switch if off.

Adele   I'm watching it.

Berlin *switches television off. This has obviously happened before.*

Berlin   Fucking France fucking Spain . . . you watch too much TV. Too much utter crap. I want to talk. We used to talk. We had proper conversations. We spoke to each other . . . remember? . . . I said words and you replied to them. It's what a wife's supposed to do. It's part of the job.

Adele   . . .

Berlin   You're rusty, obviously. I'll start. How about this . . . why don't you sleep with me any more?

Adele   . . .

Berlin   Try again. I don't think you've got the hang. I ask you a question and then you think of what the answer is . . . then you say it and that's how it starts . . . a chat . . . So here we go . . . why don't you sleep with me any more?

Adele   . . .

Berlin   You have to say, I don't know, something maybe like . . .

Adele   It's because you disgust me.

Berlin   . . .

Adele   You disgust me. Like a corpse would. Turns my stomach to touch you . . . it's not your fault. I live in a graveyard, I was bound to marry a stiff.

Adele   Don't be shocked. I thought you wanted a chat. Not chatty? Why not say something like . . . how about . . . 'Adele, how can you say that,' or 'Adele . . .'

Berlin   . . . If I could . . . I . . . If I could I'd take you to whatever fucking seaside town you want. You could have window seats on the Orient Express. If I could I'd buy you a frigging flight across Persia on a magic carpet . . . But I don't have a job any more. It's how things are. Terrible.

Adele   Nothing's 'how it is'.

Berlin   What is it you think you want, Adele?. . .

. . .

Adele   Forget it, it's not you . . . There's nothing you can do about it. It's me . . . being here I feel like I'm being buried every time I look at you . . . every time I remember where I am it's like a fistful of earth falls on my face. I need to get some air, have to dig myself out.

Berlin   I can help.

Adele   You can't.

Berlin   Why not?

Adele   Because you've got no imagination. I live in the world, Berlin. A world with millions of things in . . . But not you. You're here. If you can't see it it doesn't exist. If it's over the horizon no one lives there.

Berlin   I've got my feet planted. There's nothing wrong with that. Got my heels dug in. It makes you stronger.

. . .

Let's not argue about it now.

He lamely attempts to kiss her.

Adele   I'm going out.

Berlin   Where to?

Adele   To the station.

Berlin   Why?

Adele   Don't wait up.

Berlin   You've got it wrong again, Adele. This isn't how conversation goes. You've missed the whole idea.

Adele   Bye.

Berlin   I'll wait for you . . . we'll have another conversation! Tonight. Another talk . . . I'll be here . . . Adele . . . We can make it a regular thing . . . Adele!

Express train passing.

11   Points

Fret *and* **Sava** *are on the roof.* **Katia** *and* **Adele** *are in the main hall.*

Adele   You'll like him.

Katia   How do you know?

Adele   Because I know. He's . . . one of us.

Katia   What's one of us?

Adele   I mean . . . he's . . . cosmopolitan. There's not a place in Europe Morocco hasn't seen.

Fret   The points there . . . you see . . . pre-war. I have to operate them manually.

Sava   At least with manual points you know where you are. With automated points you haven't a clue what's going on.

Fret   You've no control.

Sava   It's a disaster waiting to happen.

Fret   That's what I said. It's what I said to head office.

Sava   I'd say it myself. If I was in your shoes.

Katia   Is he reliable?

Adele   Reliable?

Katia   Will he turn us in?

Adele   I don't think so.

Katia   I don't like you telling people.

Adele   I don't see why I should keep you a secret.

Katia   I'm not supposed to be here.

Adele   Neither am I.

Katia   I'm undesirable.

Adele   I don't think so.

Katia   Everyone else does.

Fret   If they close the station, who's going to operate the points?

Sava   A computer operator in the capital. An oily suit in an office.

Fret   Exactly. A college boy.

Sava   Who's never had his hands on a piece of dirty metal in his life.

Fret   Who's never got up at six to stand at the trackside and wait for the express . . . six hundred lives in your hands on an autumn morning.

Sava   There's something spiritual about it.

Fret   Spiritual. Exactly.

Sava   Almost religious . . .

Fret   When it comes to manual points I'm orthodox. I'm a fundamentalist.

The noise of the train in the distance coming nearer.

Sava   Look, here she comes . . . see.

Fret   Beautiful. Listen . . . sshhh!

Sava   I can hear.

Fret   The sound of machinery running smoothly . . . gorgeous.

Sava   A hymn. The sound of it. A hymn to engineering.

Adele   Why can't you stay here?

Katia   They say we're economic migrants.

Adele   That's terrible. Are you?

Katia   Who knows. Economics is a big subject.

Sava   It's a funny thing, Mr Fret, but in my experience a railwayman is a railwayman wherever you go. We speak the same language, we think the same way.

Fret   When I was a boy, I saw them laying the first tracks into the town. Tracks and sleepers . . . gangs of men handling the steel and blocks.

Sava   Tito was a railwayman. My father was a railwayman.

Fret   I said to myself. That's what Europe will be. Steel and tracks and trains.

Sava   I'm a railwayman, you're a railwayman.

Fret   Steel and tracks and trains like blood muscle and arteries holding the continent together. Connecting this place with a hundred thousand other places like it from Rotterdam to Athens.

Sava   For all I know God's a railwayman.

Fret   If God was a railwayman then things would stay on track. Things would run smoothly. I'd say God works in head office. I'd say God wears a suit.

Adele   Morocco will know what to do. He'll know.

Katia   Why are you helping me? What's in it for you?

Adele   Nothing. You.

Katia   Me?

Adele   I mean . . . I'd like to come with you.

Katia   You belong here. What do you need me for?

Adele   Europe.
I want you to show me around.

Katia   You should be happy with what you've got. Stay where you fit in. Stay at home. You're lucky you've got one. I've got nothing.

Adele   But . . . you've seen things, you've travelled, . . . I've only imagined . . .

Katia   Whatever you can imagine for yourself, Adele, this continent can come up with much worse. You'll soon learn the best way is to stay where you are, keep quiet and lie low. Believe me, you're better off where you belong.

Adele   But travel broadens the mind. That's what they say . . . isn't it?

Katia   Well, they're wrong. It doesn't broaden the mind, it stretches it like skin across a tanning rack . . . a pegged skin out to dry. Each thing you see, each thing the continent coughs up for you stretches it tighter until you can't keep all the things you've seen in the same mind and the skin rips down the middle.

Morocco *arrives.*

Morocco   Someone's telling travellers' tales. Can I join in?

Adele   Morocco! You came!

Morocco   Of course.

Adele   Where have you been?

Morocco   Everywhere, across the border, down south, up north all around . . . and I've brought presents . . . look . . . dollars, marks . . . Swiss francs . . . French francs . . . the lot. And I went to Vienna.

Adele   I told you he was cosmopolitan. What was it like?

Morocco   It was all right. Who's your friend?

Adele   She's a traveller. What happened in Vienna?

Morocco   I met a woman.

Adele   Tell me more.

Morocco   What sort of traveller?

Katia   What business is it of yours?

Adele   Tell me about the woman.

Morocco   We made love. I might be able to help you.

Katia   What makes you think I need help?

Adele   Everyone loves Morocco.

Morocco (*to* **Katia**)   It's my nose.

Adele   Your nose?

Morocco   I can smell need.

Adele   What was she like?

Morocco   She was strawberry blonde with red-rimmed glasses.

Katia   What does your nose tell you about me?

Adele   Tell me more.

Katia   You need papers and a place to stay.

Adele   Tell me about the woman.

Morocco   She was hard.
It was like getting blood out of a stone.
She said I could only touch her here.

He demonstrates by putting his hand on **Katia**. **Katia** *lets it happen.*
A bargain is being struck.

Morocco   Of course I ignored her. I'm very persistent. A
good negotiator . . . I don't take no for an answer.

Katia   Can you get me papers?

Morocco   Perhaps. It depends.

Adele   How far did you go?

Morocco   I went all the way.

Katia   Do you want money?

Morocco   Money . . . I don't like money, you never know
what it's worth. I'm a trader. I deal in things.

Katia   What things?

Morocco   It depends. I have to use my nose again. I can
also smell an opportunity.

Katia   You have a very adaptable nose.

Morocco   It's my flexible friend.

Adele   The woman . . . how did you seduce her . . . what
did you do?

Morocco (*he demonstrates on* **Katia**)   At first when I touched
her she slapped my hand and put it back.

Adele   And then?

Morocco   I tried again. I was insistent.

Adele   And then?

Morocco   And then my hand stayed put. We . . .
negotiated.

Adele   He negotiated. So cosmopolitan. So civilized.

Morocco   I can't bargain on an empty stomach. Let's eat.
I know a little place in town. It's a well-kept secret. I'm a
friend of the manager. I'm sure he'll take good care of us . . .
I have my own table.

Adele   He has a table.

Morocco   The Calypso Bar. I'll be there at eight.

Katia   So will I.

Morocco   I look forward to it. It'll be a special night.

Morocco *leaves.*

Sava   I ought to thank you.

Fret   Ought you?

Sava   For letting us stay. I ought to . . .

Fret   You know . . . it's uncommon . . . in this day and age.

Sava   It is?

Fret   It's rare . . . these days. To meet a colleague. Such as yourself. Who understands. It's uncommon.

Sava   I . . . we understand trains, that's all.

Fret   I'm not a sentimental man. I'm practical. Perhaps you haven't felt welcome. I'm sorry for that.

Sava   I like a little hostility. It puts me at my ease.

Fret   I've enjoyed . . . these past few weeks. Your staying here.

Sava   It's been a privilege.

Fret   Adele doesn't care for running a station. She hasn't the . . . commitment. You've been a help.

Sava   It was my pleasure. Please. As one comrade . . . if I can use that word . . . to another . . . it was a pleasure.

Fret   When the station closes you'll have to leave.

Sava   Perhaps the station needn't close.

Fret   It's too late now. Things have gone too far.

Sava   Maybe not. We could protest.

Fret   I thought protest only made things worse.

Sava   In the yards at Knin we did it once. We staged a sit-in.

Fret   Did you get what you wanted?

Sava   No.

Fret   See.

Sava   It didn't matter. What we wanted wasn't important. We made them notice. We annoyed them.

Fret   A sit-in.

Sava   It's worth trying.

Fret   I suppose when you get to our age a sit-in is the only kind of defiance you've got the energy left for. In the office I've got comfortable chairs and there's plenty coffee. We could hold out for weeks.

Katia   The Warsaw train's coming.

Adele   I know.

Katia   Don't you want to go and see? I thought you . . .

Adele   Do you?

Katia   No.

Adele   Neither do I.

Adele   Tell me something.

Katia   What?

Adele   Anything . . . something about you.

Katia   No.

Adele   Tell me what you've seen . . .

Katia   No.

Adele   Tell me . . . tell me your life story.

Katia   I don't have a life story. I'm one of the few people left who doesn't.

Adele   Why not?

Katia   I'm a traditionalist, I like my stories to have a point.

Adele   Tell me what happened to you . . .?

Katia   Why?

Adele   I'm interested . . .

Katia   I'm not a tourist brochure. I'm not for browsing.

A pause.

Adele   I want to kiss you.

Katia   Why?

Adele   To taste.

They kiss.

Katia   What did you taste?

Adele   Forest.

Katia   I forgot to pack my toothbrush.

Adele   Foreign languages.

Katia   I've drunk coffee.

Adele   Smoke.

Katia   It's a terrible habit . . . what do you want, Adele?

Adele   Nothing . . .
you . . .
everything.

She moves to kiss her again.

Katia   Don't.

They kiss.

The train noise is building incessantly.

Sava   Here it comes. Here it comes . . .

Fret   Magnificent . . . no orchestra could sound better.

Sava   No singer could be smoother.

Fret   It's a masterpiece. It's a bloody European classic.

They can barely be heard. Express train passes.

12   Departure

The bus stop. **Billy** *is leaving. He sits with his bag at his feet.* **Horse** *and* **Berlin** *are sitting with him. It's cold.* **Horse** *is writing 'foreigners out' on the bus stop.*

Billy   . . . do you have to do that? Someone might see.

Horse   That's the idea.

Berlin   You can't stop him. He's very zealous . . . The zeal of the convert. If you stand still long enough he'll write 'foreigners out' on your forehead.

Horse   It isn't you who should be leaving, Billy. Leaving home. Forced out. You shouldn't have to go.

Billy   I'm going because I want to.

Horse   You've been driven out. You're not the only one. A lot of good men are going.

Billy   I'm going to look for work.

Horse   They give all the jobs to the Somalis and the Ethiopians. It's true.

Billy   Who's 'they', Horse?

Horse   The left.

Berlin   The dirty anarchists. The Jews and the gyppos. The blacks and the browns.

Billy   I see.

Berlin   Polluters of the nation.

Horse   We didn't used to have them, Billy, there didn't used to be foreigners here. Now we've blocks full of them. Five to a room.

Berlin   They're bound to breed. Like rats in the damp.

Billy   You should know better, Berlin.

Berlin   Better than what?

Billy   Better than to go to these meetings. Listen to that shit.

Berlin   It keeps me off the streets. Besides I like it.

Billy   Why?

Berlin   Because it's dumb.

Billy   Berlin.

Berlin   It's dumb and blunt. Because it's beautiful. Because it's better than church.

Billy   You don't believe it any more than I do. You know it's not true.

Berlin   I like believing in things that aren't true. That's what faith is.

Billy   What about the violence?

Berlin   All necessary means in defence of the faith.

Billy   Right.

Berlin   Right.

Horse   Let's not argue. Not on Billy's last day.

Berlin   I'm not arguing.

Billy   You're spouting shite.

Berlin   Fuck you.

Horse   Come on.

Berlin   What?

Horse   Don't fight. Let's not fight. We're mates. We're pals. Pals don't fight. Come on.

Berlin   Pals. Aye. Right enough. Pals.

A pause.

Billy   Funny to be leaving. Never thought I'd . . .

Berlin   Things change.

Billy   Aye. Things change.

Horse   They don't have to change.

Billy   Still. Off to the smoke. Make my fortune and that.

Berlin   You'll be a rich man.

Billy   Drive a Volvo.

Berlin   A Mercedes.

Billy   Black windows.

Berlin   A bar in the back.

Horse   You can give us lifts.

Billy   I'll buy you one of your own.

Berlin   You'll be a rich man.

Billy   You wait. One day. I'll drive up this road. And you'll all come out and say, 'Who's this? Who's this rich guy coming here? Who's in the car?' And I'll wind down the window.

Berlin   Electric.

Horse   Zzzzzzzzz.

Billy   Hello. I'm back, boys. Fancy a drink.

Horse   I've come to buy the factory.

Berlin   I've come to do the business.

Billy   The factory's fucked. (*A pause*.)
I'm buying a mansion. A dacha in the country.

Berlin   Aye, right.

Horse   A dacha?

Berlin   In the country?

Horse   Billy, I . . .

Billy   Look . . . I hate goodbyes can we just . . . I'll . . . send you a . . .

Berlin   Aye, do that . . .

Horse   . . .
. . . a postcard?

Billy   Yeah. A postcard. From . . . wherever.

Berlin   A card from wherever.

Horse   From where?

Billy   You know . . . wherever I happen to get to.

Berlin   You never know where he'll get to.

Billy   . . . you're right enough there . . . follow the old nose, that's me.

Horse   Remember we're still here if you . . . you know.

Billy   It's not easy . . . the right words and all that . . . You don't have to wait you know. Bus'll be here anytime. It's freezing.

Horse   Fucking is as well.

Berlin   Picked a day for it.

Horse *shakes* **Billy**'*s hand.*

All   Certainly picked a day for it.

Billy *goes to shake hands with* **Berlin**. *They pause. There is embarrassment. They withdraw.*

Berlin   That's the bus coming. Got your ticket?

Billy   . . .
thanks for . . .

Berlin   No problem.

Billy   I'll just go then . . . I hate . . .

Berlin   You go then.

Horse   Bus is here.

Billy *picks up his bag . . . leaves for bus.*

Billy   Cheers then.

Both   . . . Cheers.

Leaves.

Billy *waves. Reluctant to go.* **Berlin** *and* **Horse** *wave.*

Horse   I think I'll miss him, Berlin. He's a good man. Billy. Place'll be different without him.

Berlin   I won't be different, it'll be the same. A turd drying up in the sun.

Horse   . . . with Billy gone though.

Berlin   Place'll be the same.

The sound of a bus pulling away.

13   Community issues

*Adele and **Katia** in the waiting room. **Sava** and **Fret** are on the station roof. The station is now hung with banners of protest. 'Stop the closure', 'Save our station' and **Sava** is engaged in painting 'Trains not . . .' Both men are drinking bottles of **Morocco**'s vodka.*

Katia   What time is it?

Adele   I don't know.

Katia   What time is it?

Adele   I don't care.

Katia   Adele.

Adele   I want you.

Katia *grabs her wrist to look at her watch.*

Katia   Be serious. Twenty past seven.

*She lets go of **Adele**. **Adele** remains waiting, her eyes half-closed.*

Katia   I've got forty minutes.

Sava   Fret?

Fret   What?

Sava   What rhymes with trains?

Fret   . . . Brains . . . Cranes . . . Drains . . .

Sava   No, it has to be something we don't want . . . Trains not . . . um . . .

Fret   . . . Lanes?

Sava   Lanes?

Fret   As in . . . motorway . . . lanes . . .

Sava   I don't think so.

Fret   Trains not . . . does it have to rhyme?

Sava   It's no use having a slogan if it doesn't rhyme. No one'll take you seriously.

Fret   It hardly seems to matter.

Sava   It does. It's like a good acronym. You have to have one if you're going to protest in this day and age. Without an acronym, a rhyming slogan and a concerned actress you'll be ignored.

Fret   Haven't you noticed?

Sava   What?

Fret   We're supposed to be protesters and no one's turned up. The trains have stopped stopping. The change has taken place. On the quiet. Without ceremony. There's no one out there . . . no audience, no officials . . . no one but the wolves to read the slogans. So it doesn't matter whether it rhymes or not. Does it?

Sava   It matters to me. Literary integrity. That sort of thing. I don't mind if anyone's listening. It gives me pleasure for it to be said properly. That's enough.

Katia   Show me where the Calypso Bar is. Draw me a map.

Adele   I'll take you.

Katia   It's business.

Adele   You're getting fake papers? You're moving on. Morocco told me. I'm in the know.

Katia   So what.

Adele   . . . I've got papers too. Let me travel with you.

Katia   No.

Adele   Why not?

Katia   I don't need extra baggage. I'm going alone.

Adele   We could be travelling companions. The two of us . . .

Katia   It's not the grand tour.

Adele   We could jump the trains together. We could fuck in the toilets when the conductor passes.

Katia   Use your brain, Adele.

Adele   I am. I'm using my imagination.

Katia   We fucked once.

Adele   Twice.

Katia   You've got some sort of . . . pathetic crush on me, that's all.

Adele   Katia.

Katia   We fucked. Maybe we shouldn't have. Maybe I should have left you alone. But we fucked. It was something to do while I waited for a train.

. . .

I owe you nothing. People fuck all the time. It means nothing.

Adele   Yes.

Katia   Just forget it. For God's sake don't turn it into a tragedy.

Adele   No.

Katia   I don't belong here. I have to get out. You live here. It's your place.

Adele   Yes.

Katia   I like you, Adele. It might surprise you but I like you.

Adele   Good.

Katia   God knows why.

Adele   God knows.

Katia   Things happen between people. Things happen and then they stop. Like a summer cold. Trains pass. You can't just attach yourself to someone and leave. You can't do it. Your place is here, Adele. Believe me. I know.

Long pause.

Adele   I was born here by mistake. I didn't choose it. It happened to me.
Like a car accident.
You think you know me but you don't. You don't know the first thing about me.
I'm not what you think I am, Katia.
You've never seen me before.

Katia   No.

Adele   You've lost your home and I've never had one. So we're both exiles.
. . .
Besides. I don't need to ask you. I only asked you out of politeness. I'll come anyway. I'll follow you anyway. You won't lose me.

Katia   You're very persistent.

Adele   You're very stubborn.

Katia   I don't want a puppy. If I wanted a puppy I'd buy one. You'd have to look after yourself.

Adele   I already do.

Katia   It would be your problem if you got into trouble.

Adele   It always is.

Katia   It's not Club Med.

Adele   I don't expect Club Med.

Katia   Just don't expect anything, Adele. Don't imagine things'll be like anything . . . don't expect anything except rain and policemen and stinking suburbs that look the same wherever you are.

Adele   I expect nothing.

Berlin *has arrived. Unnoticed.*

Katia   I have to go. I've got to meet Morocco.

Adele   Will you come back here later?

Katia   I don't have anywhere else to go . . .

Adele   Katia . . .

They kiss. Uneasily. Not yet resolved. **Katia** *notices* **Berlin**. *She leaves.* **Berlin** *lets her pass.*

Adele   You.

Berlin   Me.

Adele   What do you want?

Berlin   Where's Fret?

Adele   He's on the roof. Protesting.

Berlin   About what?

Adele   About the station.

Berlin   It's a bit late for that, isn't it? It's been weeks since a train stopped here.

Adele   It keeps him happy. What's going on, Berlin?

Berlin   Where's your friend gone, Adele?

Adele   I don't know what you're talking about.

Berlin   FRET!

Adele   What's going on?

Berlin *almost accidently kicks some of* **Katia**'s *things.*

Berlin   Things have got a bit cluttered in here.

Adele   What?

Berlin   Messy. You know. Litter. Rubbish.

Adele   Where?

Berlin   Here . . . there and everywhere I'd say. Look . . . the floor . . . the station unkempt . . . just look out at the square . . . pride of the town it used to be . . .

Adele   You're losing me.

Berlin   Do you remember how people used to stroll in the sunshine? Drink coffee outdoors . . . watch the world go by . . . everything neat, everything in order.

Adele   So . . .

Berlin   Look at it now.

Adele   It's nearly winter. No one's going to sit outdoors.

Berlin   Grass verges untended. The road left pot-holed and crumbling at the edges . . . Vagrants under the trees . . . strange faces at the bar counter.

Adele   Berlin?

Berlin   I've got time on my hands, Adele. I notice the little things.

Adele   Is this you and Horse . . . is this your little group . . .?

Berlin   I want to discuss community issues . . . that's all . . . A bit of tidying up we want done. We've had a meeting. It's been agreed.

Adele   Who, Berlin? Who?

Berlin   The community. FRET!

Adele   Which community? I wasn't there.

Fret *enters.* **Horse** *has appeared behind* **Sava** *and suddenly grabs him, covering his mouth. He begins to punch the older man on the stomach and face methodically and quietly.*

Berlin   There you are, Fret.

Fret   What do you want?

Berlin   I'm here on behalf of a . . . on behalf of the community, Fret. To hand over a petition . . . we've all signed it . . . People are frightened, Fret, frightened and upset.

Fret   Are they?

Berlin   Because when they pass their once beloved old station they find it's been turned into some sort of hostel for the homeless.

Fret   The station's closed. You'ld think people would be concerned about that.

Berlin   Not just vagrancy, Fret, but prostitutes seem to be operating out of here. Gypsy prostitutes. It's not on, Fret. It's affecting the women.

Fret   The station's shut. No longer in operation.

Berlin   I think we're all sorry about that, Fret. Like I said, I've brought a petition. Just to say . . . well . . . If they're not gone soon . . .

Fret   Get out.

Berlin   I probably don't have to tell you that . . . there's unruly elements in the town . . . you know . . . hotheads etc. I hate to be the bringer of bad news but . . .

Fret   Is this a threat? I'll call the police.

Sava *has gone limp.* **Horse** *lets him drop. He stands above him holding his fist which is now sore. He sucks his fist.*

Horse   You cunt.

Berlin   Do.

Horse   Bloody old hard-boned cunt.

Berlin   Do that.

Horse   Hurt my fist.

Horse *gives* **Sava** *a desultory kick, then leaves.*

Berlin   I wouldn't want something as worrying as this to pass them by unnoticed . . . only you know as well as I do that these people don't take a warning. They get fuelled up and there's no stopping them. I'm just saying . . .

Fret   What?

Berlin   I'm just saying that . . . it worries me. I'm worried.

Fret Not sleeping?

Berlin I suggest you tell your friends . . . for their own safety as much as anything . . .

Fret You concern yourself with your friends and I'll worry about mine.

Berlin Good.

Fret Like I said, the station's closed.

Berlin Well, then, bad deed done, tale told, time to go. I'll see you at home, Adele.

Adele I don't think so.

Berlin Later then.

Adele I think I'm staying here tonight.

Berlin Right . . . later then.

Express train passing.

14 Local songs

Inside the Calypso Bar. As before, **Morocco** *is sitting with* **Katia**. **Morocco** *has been drinking. We can hear a group of men singing nationalist songs in the meeting room.*

Morocco I pity them. Locals. I pity them. They're like dogs whose owners' died . . . hungry dogs lying across their masters' grave and whining to the night . . . they stay in one cold spot and wait to starve. I pity them.

Katia I think we ought to go . . .

Morocco Whereas yourself . . . you and me . . . I think . . .

Katia Finish your drink . . . we'll go outside.

Morocco I think we're familiar with bigger things than these louts. We're familiar with cities . . . we've crossed

borders . . . We're at home only when we're away from home
. . . Here . . . we'll have a toast . . . to leaving home . . .

Katia   . . . will you quiet down.

Morocco   To refugees. That stuff you said about losing
your home . . . you were lucky. It was a blessed release . . .
nothing's more of a prison than a home. Nothing is a bigger
threat to a man's liberty than three meals a day and familiar
faces at the dinner table. To Freedom!

Berlin *has entered from where songs are being sung and observes the
scene. While* **Katia** *speaks,* **Morocco** *is kissing her hand.*

Katia   Don't mistake me, Morocco. I'm not a trader or a
traveller by nature. I'm a coward. The way you see my eyes
glance is me checking the exits. I'm not a free spirit.

Morocco   Yes you are . . . You're like the breeze . . . you
move like a dancer.

Katia   I fidget. I try not to give snipers a chance to set their
sights. (*Indicating a roomful of singers.*)
I would like to leave now.

Morocco   Like love, you never stay too long in one place.

Katia   If I seem in a hurry to leave it's because people who
stay too long in one place get noticed. People who get noticed
get punished.

Songs of the men build up.

Express train passing.

15   This is nice

Adele *on the station roof. She is reading her brochures.* **Berlin**
arrives noticeably drunk.

Berlin   Do you know what time it is?

Adele   . . .

Berlin   You're supposed to be at home.

Adele   I'm here.

Berlin   I was worried. I've been worried about you.

Adele   Why?

Berlin   Something could have happened to you. Anything could have happened. I was worried.

Adele   Go home, Berlin. I'm waiting for someone.

Berlin   It's past midnight. Who are you waiting for at this time . . . the trains have stopped.

Adele   Fuck you.

Berlin   Who?

Adele   Just someone.

Berlin   Maybe they'll be late.

Adele   What?

Berlin   Who you're waiting for? Maybe they've been held up.

Adele   Maybe.

Berlin   Maybe they've been delayed . . .

Adele   Berlin?

Berlin   I told you . . . anything can happen.
I don't like to worry you but it's the way things are at the moment.
Terrible.

Adele   What are you talking about?

Berlin   Who knows.

Adele   Where have you been tonight?

Berlin   Out with some mates.

Adele   Where? Out where?

Berlin   In town.

Adele   There isn't an 'in town' here, Berlin, there's the Calypso and the street.

Berlin   We were in town.

Adele   You've torn your jeans.

Berlin   That was careless.

Adele   They were new.

Berlin   Trust a woman to notice.

Adele   Your shirt . . .

Berlin   Stop nagging, Adele, you're not my mother.

Adele   There's spots of blood.

Berlin   Boys will be boys. We were out on the town we weren't collecting for charity.

Adele   Thought you'd hit her, like you hit her dad?

Berlin   She oughtn't to be out so late. It's risky.

Adele   Who?

Berlin   Who?

Adele   Who oughtn't be out so late?

Berlin   Nobody. Anybody . . . everybody.

Adele   You said she.

Berlin   Did I? Come on. Come home with me. Let's get home.

Adele   Don't touch me.

Berlin   We just got a bit pissed.
She was in the alley . . .
She was fucking Morocco in the alley by the Calypso.
Like a dog.
Disgusting.

Adele   What did you do to her?

Berlin   Nothing.

Adele   Tell me.

Berlin   We just got a bit pissed. That's all. He wanted a fight as much as us. It was disgusting, fucking gypsies in a back alley. This town needs cleaning up. Billy was right. It's going under.

Adele   Tell me what you did . . .

Berlin   We gave Morocco a doing.

Adele   You . . .

Berlin   It's a boys' thing. I knew you wouldn't understand.

Adele   . . .

A very tense pause. **Adele**'s *anger is so great that she can't speak. She can't move, she's immobilised.*

Berlin   I'm sorry.
I said sorry.
What else can I say? It's done now . . . he'll be all right. It was just a gesture. I'll speak to him in the morning. In the morning, I'll have a word . . . sort it out. He'll be all right about it. I know Morocco. He knows it wasn't personal.
. . .
We need to talk, Adele.
We should talk.
Adele.

Adele   . . .

Berlin   . . . it feels to me like you've been . . . distant . . . lately. Somewhere else.

Adele   . . .

Berlin   I can't seem to get through. I can't seem to make a connection.

Adele   . . .

Berlin   I'm not as bad as you think, Adele. I'm not like Horse, I'm not like the other guys. I can feel it when there's a problem between us. I can sense it.

Adele   Go home, Berlin.

Berlin   I just want to say something.

Adele   Go home before I push you on the track.

Berlin   This is important.

Adele   I'm not listening.

He holds her.

Berlin   But you have to listen. I have to tell you . . . (*She struggles a little, he pauses, he waits till she is still before saying.*) I love you.

Adele   Berlin.

Berlin   Kiss me.

Adele   Let go of me.

Berlin   I'm worried about you . . .
We need to talk.
I don't want to let go of you . . .

Adele   Get off.

Berlin   I feel as though if I let go I could lose you. I want to squeeze you tight. I love you, Adele, I don't want you to leave.

Adele   Berlin!

Berlin   This is nice.

Adele   You're hurting.

Berlin   A chance to . . . touch . . .

Adele   . . . you're not like this.

Berlin   . . . we need to explore each other more . . .

Adele   Let me go now.

Berlin *forces her to the floor. He puts his hand over her mouth.*

Berlin   Where's there to go? At this time of night . . .
We've got the evening to ourselves . . . a crisp autumn evening all to ourselves. A still night . . . not a sound. Shhh! can you hear? My voice is echoing in the forest . . .

16 Solidarity

Fret *and* **Sava** *in the station waiting room.* **Sava** *is nursing his wounds. Meanwhile, in the street near the Calypso* **Morocco** *staggers and falls, brutally beaten.*

Sava   What are you thinking about?

Fret   What's happening to things, Sava?

Sava   Is it the station?

Fret   Not just the station, not just us but . . . everywhere I look . . . It feels like things are crumbling . . . I've lived in this town all my life. Since I was a boy I've never been anywhere else. I've seen buildings go up and come down, I've seen street names change . . . it's formed around me like geology. And now it's wearing away. It's eroding in the wind. Losing tiny particles of substance every day, getting smaller, breaking up.

Sava   You're upset. Berlin's upset you. Believe me, I've seen it before.

Fret   I didn't know what to say to him. I just . . . stood.

Sava   When there's nothing to say, silence is at least a dignified response.

Fret   But I let him . . . say those things about this town. I just stood. Let it happen.

Sava   If people want to know the truth about this town they only need to come here. They'll soon see it's not the way Berlin wants it. People only need to turn up.

Fret   They won't be able to find it. They'll just see a blur from the train. Express trains going so fast they can't even make out the station name as they pass. That's all that'll be left of us. The home you thought you had, the place you thought you came from, the person you thought you were . . . whoosh! Whooosh! Gone past. Dust on the breeze. By the time they think to turn up it'll already be gone.

Katia *arrives and sees* **Morocco.** *He is regaining consciousness painfully.* **Katia** *is smoking.*

Katia   I ran away. I hid. If you were wondering.

Morocco   I know.

Katia   I'm sorry.

Morocco   What for?

Katia   For you. Sorry you got hit.

Morocco   Thank you.

Katia   I'm not sorry I ran away.

Morocco   Don't be.

Katia   I would have brought help but . . . you know . . .

Morocco   I know.

Katia   I don't like to deal with the police. I feel uncomfortable with uniforms of any kind, the police especially.

Morocco   Don't explain.

Katia   There was no point in me staying. I wouldn't have been any use.

Morocco   None.

Katia   They'd have only got more excited. If I'd stayed. I'd have been a prize . . . of some kind . . . they think that way. It happens, I've seen it. Once they've tasted blood . . . you know . . . sharks, they're like sharks.

Morocco   You did the right thing. I'm glad you're safe.

Katia's *hardness crumbles slightly. She crouches beside him.*

Katia   Your nose . . . it's bleeding . . . I wouldn't have been any use. My fists are like sponges. I can't fight.

Morocco   Did you see? Did you see who they were?

Katia   I heard. I couldn't see.

Morocco   What did you hear?

Katia   Thumping. A lot of thumps.

Morocco (*a moment of utterly impotent rage*)   I'll kill the fucking little shits, I'll fucking . . .

Katia   I didn't see who they were. I'm sorry. It seemed more important to hide.

Morocco   Just local boys . . . could have been any of them . . . probably all of them. I didn't see. There were a few.

Katia   You were lucky . . . by the looks of it. You got away lightly.

Morocco   At least they didn't have knives.

Katia   Every cloud has a silver lining.

Morocco   You've still got the papers? The passports?

Katia   I made sure.

Morocco   I must have looked a fucking prick. Trousers down in the shit . . .

Katia   Don't think about it.

Morocco   They got their money's worth out of me. I gave them a good show.

Katia   Try and forget it.

Morocco   I remember seeing the rings on his fist . . . I remember just the smallest part of a second having time to think. Fuck. Oh fuck.

Katia   Shhh.

Morocco   In the moment between turning round and his fist connecting with my nose. I had time to think . . . fuck, there's four of them . . . I thought fuck, my trousers are round my ankles . . . and I thought fuck he's wearing rings.

Katia   I'm sorry I ran away.

Morocco   After that my recollection's a bit hazy . . . you understand.

Katia   I can imagine. I don't need the details.

Morocco No.

Katia I know we're supposed to stick together people like us. I know it's expected.

Morocco I didn't expect it.

Katia It's just . . . I've found solidarity often just means more people get hurt . . . and what's the point of that?

Morocco I was the unlucky one this time. Next time it could be you . . . then I'd run away.

Katia Exactly. Best take your turn and hope for the best. It's not very life affirming, is it?

Morocco Sometimes life's not very life affirming.

Katia No. Your nose . . . poor Morocco.

Morocco (*winces*) Please . . . I'm fine. I think it would be best if we got off the streets.

Katia If you still want to fuck . . . you did pay after all. I've got my passports . . . we still have a deal?

Morocco I don't feel like it.

Katia No. I suppose not . . .

Morocco The day after tomorrow. A bus comes through in the afternoon. Adele'll know the time.

Katia You should get home. It's late. It's after midnight. You should have a wash . . . you don't want infections . . .

Morocco I will.

Katia I'm sorry I ran away.

Morocco I know. I'd have done the same. In your shoes I'd have done the same.

Express train passing.

17   Foreigners out

The bus stop. **Horse**'s *earlier writing of 'foreigners out' remains. It's very cold.* **Katia, Adele** *and* **Sava** *are waiting for a bus. It's dark and quiet. Although there is obviously a great deal of emotion none is shown or expressed except in* **Katia**'s *holding of her father's hand.* **Sava**'s *face shows the signs of his recent beating. After some moments a bus arrives.*

18   Blame

Fret *is sitting in a comfortable chair.* **Sava** *stands nearby.*

Sava   She went.

Fret   They go eventually. It's . . . inevitable.

Sava   You're right. It's not a comfort though, is it? That it's inevitable?

Fret   No.

Sava   I think she considers me to blame.

Fret   For what?

Sava   . . .
Most of it.
She blames me for protesting, here, she says we drew unnecessary attention to ourselves.
Brought down the fists upon myself, she thinks.
Probably right.
Still, that's not what hurts.

Fret   The face?

Sava   The face? My face?

Fret   Does it hurt?

Sava   No, it's numb. I'm a little drunk so it's numb. It's not my face that hurts but that she blames me for the other thing.

Fret   What other thing . . .?

Sava The past.

Fret You're not responsible . . .

Sava The war, you know . . .

Fret It's not your fault, surely.

Sava You know they . . . She was . . . assaulted. She was . . . A lot of people were assaulted . . . but . . . I think she was . . . She never says but I think . . . she blames me for making her stay, making her stay so that what happened to her could happen to her. I thought it was our duty as citizens not to desert our homes. As a result . . .

Fret You can't have known . . .

Sava Perhaps I did know. Looking back, I think I probably did. But I'm, by nature, a person who stays. I'm not sorry. I'm sorry she blames me but I'm not sorry that we stayed. By staying I think we brought a sliver of dignity, a sliver of civilization to an otherwise damned place. We can't leave places to the wolves. Still, dignity always costs something. I think she blames me.

Fret You decided not to go with her this time?

Sava I've found myself here. In a station. A station is a place to finish a journey as well a place to start one.

Fret I'm glad you made that decision.

19 Wolves

Berlin *and* **Horse**. **Fret** *and* **Sava** *in the station.*

Berlin The radio said it was the coldest October night for a decade and a half. There wasn't a cloud, just the dark and the stars. Horse kept saying he wished he'd brought a hat. He should have brought a hat . . . and he kept rubbing his ears . . . anyway we'd soon be warm enough . . . Did you bring the vodka?

Horse Of course I did.

Berlin   Of course he had. Of course he'd brought the vodka. It was the coldest October night for a decade and a half and the vodka left a beautiful burn around the heart. A burn that spread out across the chest, oiling the veins and arteries, loosening muscles, heating nerve ends . . .

Horse   Berlin, I've . . . (*Hiccup.*) shi . . . (*Hiccup.*)

Berlin   Shhh.

Horse   I've got the hiccups.

Berlin   Shh.

Horse   I've got the fucking hiccups. (*Laughing.*)

Berlin   Hold your breath.

Horse *draws in breath.*

Berlin   Put your head between your legs.

Horse *puts his head between his legs.*

Berlin   One two three . . .

Although not asleep, **Fret** *and* **Sava** *have been in a waking dream.*

Fret   Shhh! Did you hear something?

Sava   Hmmm?

Fret   Shhh.
. . .
Do you hear?
A giggling . . . a giggling

Sava   I heard something . . . a rustling . . . I'm not sure I'd call it a giggling though.

Fret   I'd swear . . . maybe not a giggle but something like a giggle.

Sava   You were dreaming. You just heard voices in your dream.

Fret   You're probably right. I've been soaking in the vodka too long. What time's it?. . .

Sava (*looking at station clock*)   It's late. Or early . . .
depending how you look at it.

Fret (*looking at station clock*)   I'd say it was late. I must have
drifted off. It's cold.

Sava   Bitter.

Fret   We should go inside. I've made you up a bed in the
office.

Sava   A little longer. It's a beautiful night. We'll finish the
bottle.

Horses *stands, exhales.*

Berlin   Fifty. And again.

Horse *takes in a deep breath, holds it and bends double again.*

Fret   Wait a minute. I heard it again.

. . .
I heard voices.
I'm sure of it.

Sava   Sure . . .?

Fret   No.

Horse *lets out a huge breath.*

Fret   What was that?

Berlin   Come on . . . Hurry up.

Horse   I can hear voices inside.

Berlin   Give me the matches. It's fucking freezing, my
hands are shaking, look. (*His hands are shivering.*) I am fucking
freezing, Jesus Christ, give us a nip.

Horse   Shut up. Shut up, they'll hear us.

Berlin   Christ, I can't light the frigging match. I can't light
the match. My hands are jelly give us a nip. Give us a fucking
nip. (*He takes a swig of vodka.*)

Fret   Probably wolves.

Sava   Wolves?

Fret   There's a pack in the forest. They crossed the forest when the border came down.

Sava   They came back to the hills near our town after the war started. You could hear them howling in the suburbs. Horrible.

Fret   I used to hate it . . . being on my own. On nightshift. I don't like the dark.

Sava   Me neither.

Fret   I used to ask myself what I was afraid of. Who'd want to attack a stationmaster? I hadn't any money to rob.

Sava   So what were you afraid of?

Fret   That's just it. I could never pin it down. Animals . . .? It might have been the forest, the dark or even the trains.

Sava   What's there to be scared of in a train?

Fret   You don't know what it's bringing you. You don't know what it's going to take away.

Berlin   It's lit. Throw it.

Horse   What?

Sava   I heard something that time.

They both listen.

Horse *lights a cloth and stick it into the top of a bottle.*

Berlin   . . . Fucking throw it.

Horse   Wait a minute!

Berlin   What?

Fret   Come on, we'll go inside.

Sava   Too cold to be out here.

Fret   Yes. Too cold. Yes. It's probably nothing anyway.

Sava   Probably nothing at all.

Berlin   Come on!

Horse   Where?

Berlin   What?

Horse   Where? Throw it where?

Berlin   I don't care.

Horse   It's going to explode.

Berlin   I don't know where.

Horse   It's going to explode.

Berlin   Anywhere. In there.

Horse   But I heard voices.

Berlin   Fuck the voices. (*He takes the bottle from* **Horse**.)

Horse   Berlin!

Berlin   So I threw it.

Fret *is in the office.* **Sava** *on his way.*

Sava   It's just imagination, Fret. If there's one thing I learned in the yards about staying awake on a long night it's keep the old imagination under control. Don't let the old mind invent things to frighten itself. Don't conjure up demons. Don't talk to ghosts.

Berlin   There was just the smallest moment of total silence and we saw the little flame curve through the air . . . then the familiar sound; the pleasant, reassuring sound of bottle on concrete and the flame taking. We ran. We ran into the forest.

Horse   Oh Christ Jesus God cunt fuck.

Berlin   From the forest we stood and watched it go up. It seemed like seconds to me. Less than seconds. Like a bomb. There was no stopping it. On the news the fireman said the station was a tinderbox. He said it was criminal. Criminal that it could have been left in that condition. They didn't have a chance he said. No one stood a chance in that place. Criminal.

LOOK AT IT LOOK AT IT LOOK AT IT! . . . IT'S BEAUTIFUL.

At first we just saw the light inside. Just an orange glow inside
and then some smoke. It was a clear night so we could see the
smoke rising. Even from that distance we could feel it warm.
AMAZING. (*He holds out the back of his hand.*)
I CAN FEEL IT. I CAN FEEL IT FROM HERE!
It was comforting. The heat. The light. The timbers
cracking. Like working the furnace. Like standing next to a
brazier on the night shift.

*The noise of a train is beginning slowly in the distance. However it is,
at least initially, imperceptible, growing during the rest of the speech.*

The express train passes . . . this time however the noise continues.

20   Europe

Adele *and* **Katia** *are in the toilets on an international train.* **Katia**
is sitting on the toilet. **Adele** *has opened the window and is looking out.*

Katia   He'll be all right. Won't he? He'll register and . . .
Fret was good about things . . . Fret was a godsend. He likes
company. Dad needs company.

Adele   Where are we going to go to first?

Katia   It's your town. You know it, what it's like. Will he
be all right?

Adele   Let's go to Berlin . . . for the cabaret.

Katia   I said he should come with us but he's tired of
travelling.

Adele   Vienna. Vienna for the cakes.

Katia   And it's easier when you're on your own . . . to go
unnoticed. To look after yourself. To slip past guards . . . It's
best he stayed. He seemed happy. Did you think he was
happy?

Adele   Portugal. I never even thought of Portugal.

Katia   I feel responsible. He needs looking after.

Adele   Come and look . . . come and look out the window.

Katia   Are we out of the forest?

Adele   Not yet, do you know which way we're going?

Katia   West.

Adele   Which mountains are we in?

Katia   I don't know.

Adele   It doesn't matter. We're in mountains.

Katia   It was the right thing to leave. That's the main thing. It was the right decision.

Adele   Paris . . . we'll go to Paris . . . for the romance . . . (*Kisses* **Katia** *briefly.*) Milan . . . we'll go to Milan.

Katia   Maybe.

Adele   Or Prague . . .

Katia   Perhaps.
. . . Perhaps . . . if you think about it . . . I suppose we were lucky to be blown into your station . . . perhaps it was just as well . . .

Adele   Just as well? . . . It was the best thing that ever happened.

Katia   I'm not sure I would go so far as to say that.

Berlin   The next day, after the fire, the government minister came to see the ashes. He said they would stamp us out. He said . . . these monsters aren't part of our nation. They don't belong in our midst. He said we have to drive them out. There's no place for them here. No place for them anywhere.

Adele   We'll go to Moscow . . .

Katia   We could go to Petersburg.

Berlin   The country has been sitting on a powderkeg for too long. A spark was bound to catch. He said he'd tighten up on immigration controls. After all . . . feelings were running high all over the continent.

Adele *kisses* **Katia**. **Katia** *finally kisses back. They begin to kiss sexually. Their hands exploring each other.*

Adele   To Venice.

Katia   To Rome.

Berlin   He said it was a tragedy. A terrible tragedy. And he said he was making a ministerial visit. The problems were being considered at the highest level.

Katia   To Rotterdam.

Adele   To Copenhagen.

Berlin   We were on the television . . . on the front of magazines. Me and Horse, we were discussed on the radio. Protest songs were written about us.

Adele   Sofia.

Katia   Budapest.

Berlin   They said the name of our town, politicians and sociologists all across the continent said its name.

Adele   Barcelona.

Katia   Marseilles.

Berlin   Until it wasn't a name any more but a condition, not a place but an effect.
But it was our town.

Adele   Athens.

Katia   Hamburg.

Berlin   For one day, for one week . . . maybe even for a month. Everyone knew the name of our town. And now they know. They know that even as they travel to some older . . .

Adele   Salzburg.

Berlin   Or more beautiful . . .

Katia   Sarajevo.

Berlin   Or more important place.

Adele   Just imagine.

Katia   Shh . . .

Berlin   They know that, in our own way, we're also
Europe.

*Lights down . . . the noise of the train continues for a few moments in
the dark.*

The Architect

For Mum, Dad and Mike

No Matter. Try again.
Fail Again. Fail Better.

Samuel Beckett

'The Smoke'

A little house among trees by the lake
From the roof smoke rises
Without it
How dreary would be
House, trees and lake.

Bertolt Brecht

The Architect was first performed at the Traverse Theatre, Edinburgh, on 23 February 1996. The cast was as follows:

Leo Black	Alexander Morton
Martin Black	Tom Smith
Sheena Mackie	Una McLean
Paulina Black	Morag Hood
Dorothy Black	Ashley Jensen
Joe	Eric Barlow
Billy	Paul Hickey

Directed by Philip Howard
Designed by Simon Vincenzi
Lighting by Chahine Yavroyan
Music by Reuben Taylor

Characters

Leo Black, *an architect, fifties.*
Paulina Black, *his wife, forties.*
Martin Black, *his son, twenties.*
Dorothy Black, *his daughter, twenties.*
Joe, *a lorry driver, forties.*
Billy, *a young man, twenties.*
Sheena Mackie, *a campaigner, fifties.*

Setting: A city. The present.

Act One

1

Darkness.
The long blast of a siren.
A moment of silence.
A series of explosions.
Large buildings falling to the ground.
A crowd applauding.

2

A summer afternoon.
A building site.

A small trestle table stands centre stage. On the table are architectural plans and blueprints. The papers are weighted down with stones to stop them blowing away. Two hard hats are on the table.

Martin *is looking casually at the blueprints.*
Leo *enters carrying an architectural model, it is bulky, he is struggling with it.* **Martin** *looks.*

Leo Some professions, Martin, exist only or mainly, to provide particular people with a congenial way of earning their living. Publishing, for example, or radio, you mentioned radio. These people, these publishers and so on, they're interesting. I've met them sometimes. They're creative people. Their surroundings are, if you like, seductive. But in the end, these are people without effect in the world. Do you see what I'm saying. They have no . . . power to shape, no responsibility. Now, building, construction, engineering, architecture . . . these have effects. Here you have responsibility. Obviously you can dream, use your imagination, of course, but there's a purpose . . . you put your dreams on paper . . . blueprints, drawings.

Your smallest line, the merest gesture of the pencil, can be the curve of a motorway flyover, or pull a tower up from the slums, or shape a square from a mess of alleys. That's what we do, Martin, we dream these structures and then ...

Martin   It's flat.

Leo   Sorry?

Martin   This. Here. I thought you built. I thought you were a builder. This is flat.

Leo   This is the car park. It's supposed to be flat.

Martin   Oh.

Leo   To go back, we dream these structures, these buildings and ...

Martin   You said there was going to be a tower. There's a tower on the model.

Leo   ... the buildings take shape, become solid ...

Martin   There's no tower here.

Leo   ... people live in them, work in them ...

Martin   There's some lumps.

Leo   We have an effect. You understand?

Martin *refers to the model.*

Martin   Nothing like that.

Leo   The tower's going to be over there. At the head of the docks. Where the fish market used to be. They're still digging foundations. But you can imagine ...

Martin   Is this one of yours? The tower? Did you dream it?

Leo   A lot of people are involved on the project.

Martin   Did you think it up though? Your dream?

Leo   I'm part of the design team, obviously ... so in that sense, yes. Everyone has their role, everyone has input.

Martin   What's your input?

Leo   Well, the car park's mine . . . my job on the team is access. So clearly . . . parking . . . which is important on a project like this . . . also security . . . the walls, if you like.

Martin   They're big.

Leo   Well spotted.

Martin   Thick.

Leo   Look around you, Martin . . . beyond the fencing, over there . . . what do you see?

Martin   Houses. Some people.

Leo   Houses, yes, but . . . look at the immediate environment . . . the surroundings . . .

Martin   . . .

Leo   Understand? This site's in the middle of no-man's-land. Look at it. Devastation. Someone in the planning department told me, this is officially third world status. Which means vandalism, burglars, and Christ knows whatever else. It's a prime example . . .
You dream up ideas, but you have to think, you have to see potential problems. Solve them. Before they happen . . . understand? . . . I saw the problem . . . that . . . and this is the physical solution.

Martin   Big walls.

Leo   Metaphorically, yes, I suppose so.

Martin   How high?

Leo   Four metres, plus barbed wire . . .

Martin   The tower. How high?

Leo   Square footage?

Martin   How many floors?

Leo   Seventeen.

Martin   How high can you build something?

Leo   In what way do you mean high?

Martin   Up the way high? How high can a thing be built? Anything?

Leo   It's an interesting question.

Martin   Interesting.

Leo   Design, materials and nature are what you have to think about. A good design can take poor materials higher. Good materials can support a poor design. And then there's nature – wind, damp, heat, earthquakes . . . the imponderables . . . you overcompensate for nature . . .

Martin   How high then?

Leo   The base of the building would have to be wide . . . to support the height. Lifts are a problem, over a certain number of floors and you need separate lifts . . . then there's the human elements . . . vertigo. People do get vertigo. I suppose that counts as nature. Materials, design and nature . . . if one of these factors is out of harmony then, when you get beyond a certain point, the structure overbalances, things get dangerous. You can work it out. Theoretically, though, there's no limits.

Martin   Can you build a thing high enough that if you fell off you wouldn't hit the ground?

Leo   . . .

Martin   High enough so that if you fell, you'd fall into orbit?

Leo   This is offices, Martin. No one's going to fall out.

Martin   Could you though?

Leo   Is this a joke?

Martin   I'm only asking how . . .

Leo   It feels like you're making a joke.

Martin   I'm not, honestly.

Leo   I thought you wanted to talk about work.

Martin   I was.

Leo   If you're bored . . .

Martin   I'm not bored . . . I was asking a question.

Leo   It sounded like a joke. I'm sorry. I didn't . . .

Martin   Doesn't matter. Forget it.

Leo   Put this on.

Leo *gives* **Martin** *a hard hat.*

Martin   What for?

Leo   Safety. It's to protect your head.

Martin   From what?

Leo   Everyone on site has to wear a hard hat. It's regulations.

Martin   But there's nothing above us. It's flat. Only lumps.

Leo   We're on site, Martin. Accidents happen. You'll wear a hard hat.

Martin   I'm just saying . . .

Leo   What the hell is the problem with you?
There's no pain in wearing it.
It won't hurt your head.
I said to put it on.

Martin *puts the hat on.*

Martin   I look like one of the Village People.

Leo   What?

Martin   Doesn't matter.

Leo   You mutter, Martin, do you know that? You're a mutterer. Under your breath. You speak behind your hand. Do you notice yourself doing it?

Martin (*muttering*)   No.

Leo   If you've got something to say. Say it clearly.
Make the point.
. . .
You have to think about your presentation.

Think about how you come across.

. . .

He offers **Martin** *a cigarette.*

Martin   I don't smoke.

Leo   Quite right too.

He tries to light his cigarette. He can't get the lighter to work.

Too windy.

He turns and cups his hand. The lighter still doesn't work.

Damn.

He lifts his jacket to use as a windbreak. Again he fails.

Damn.

Martin   I thought you'd given up.

Leo   Not yet.

Martin   Mum said she didn't let you smoke in the house any more.

Leo   We're not in the house.

Martin   Die if you want to.

Leo   You're muttering again. Stand here.

Martin *stands in front of* **Leo** *to block the wind.*

Martin   I said, 'Die if you want to.'

Leo   Closer.

Martin *stands closer.*

Martin   Man your age. Your job. You're probably due a stroke.

Leo   Closer.

Martin *and* **Leo** *stand uncomfortably close. The cigarette is finally lit.* **Martin** *moves away.*

Leo   So. What do you think?

Martin   About what?

Leo The work. Does it appeal?

Martin . . . ?

Leo Are you interested or not?

Martin . . . ?

Leo Do you want the job?

Martin What job?

Leo What do you think I've been talking about?

Martin I don't know. Stuff.

Leo I wanted you to see the work.
I'm offering you a job, Martin.
You don't do anything . . . you're drifting . . . you don't . . .
I've been thinking, for a while now, just the time hasn't been
right, I've been considering the idea of setting up on my own.
Small scale. Nothing big, not yet anyway. It's only an idea at
the moment but this job's coming to an end and . . .
I want to get back to . . .
a certain control . . . understand?
This work, there's prestige but there's no control.

Martin Who builds the models?

Leo Never mind the model. Are you interested?

Martin You used to let me play with these, when you'd
finished with them. I put toy soldiers in the buildings . . . I
staged riots, assassinations and things, street to street
fighting, car bombs and earthquakes . . .

Leo They're technical models. They're not toys.

Martin They're so delicate. So perfect. They look solid
but you only have to nudge them and something breaks.

Leo You could have damaged them.

Martin The model's clean . . . Is that deliberate? When
you make them? They don't look anything like real
buildings. There's no dirt. No mess around them. Just white
card, patches of green felt and pretend trees. They look like

film buildings. They look as though the sun's always shining on them.

Leo   Do you want to work with me or not?

. . .

It would be a job.

Martin   Can I do the models?

Leo   You'd have to start at the bottom . . . but you'd be trained. I could start you off with . . .

Martin   I could be in charge of making the models look real. Cover the walls in graffiti or something . . . put little models of dossers under the bridges . . . Use my know-how . . . Could I do that?

Leo   Why don't we have a look at the foundations?

Martin   Whatever you say, boss . . .

Leo   You can see how the building takes shape.

Martin   Whatever you want, boss.

Sheena *has entered. She stands by the model. She is carrying some papers.*

Leo   I want to know what you want, Martin. I know what I want. I'm trying to help you.

Martin   Dad, there's . . .

Leo   I don't expect you to be interested, you know. You don't have to pretend . . . Obviously you're interested in other things. Whatever. I don't know. You don't tell me. If you told me, maybe I could get in touch with someone . . .

Martin   Foundations . . . fine. Dad . . . there's a woman . . .

Leo   You mentioned radio. Maybe I could ring someone . . .

Martin   Cheers. But . . .

Leo   I have some contacts. I just thought it was possible you'd be interested in working for me.

Martin   I said. I said I was interested.

Leo   Don't do me any favours.

Martin   All right. I'm not interested.

Leo   Well, what then? What exactly do you want?

Martin   . . .
Do you need a bicycle courier?

Sheena   Excuse me.

Leo   Sorry?

Martin   I tried to tell you.

Sheena   Mr Black?

Martin . She's been stood there waiting.

Sheena   Leo Black? Sorry to bother you. My name's
Sheena Mackie. I haven't caught you at a bad time, have I?

Leo   No . . . I'm sorry. Are you supposed to be here?

Sheena   I'll only take a minute. I've got a taxi waiting.

Leo   Do you have a site pass?

Sheena   I didn't know I needed one?

Leo   No one's allowed on site without a pass . . . I'm sorry
it's regulations . . .

Sheena   Well. I'm here now so . . . maybe we could have a
chat . . .

Leo   It's Saturday morning, Mrs . . .

Sheena   Mackie, it's actually Ms. As I say, I'll only be a
minute, the thing is I've tried to get you at your office, but
you always seem to be busy . . . I don't know if you remember
the letter? I've put a copy in with the petition.

Leo   Petition? You've lost me.

Sheena   I'm the tenants' representative. From Eden
Court.
We wrote to you about the flats weeks ago now.

Leo   What letter?
I haven't seen any . . .
Just a minute. Martin, could you get the phone from the car?

Sheena   I wouldn't normally bother you but things are moving on. We need to keep things going. For the campaign. Your wife said you'd be down here. I thought I'd take the chance to catch you.

Leo   There's obviously been some . . .
Some kind of mix up.
I'm sure we can sort it out. The thing is . . . you need a site pass. You understand we can't have people wandering round, in case there's an accident. If you hold on, my son'll ring the security people. Martin, could you give Mrs Mackie your hat. While you're on site you need a hard hat. In case anything falls on your head. For insurance . . .

Martin *gives her his hat.*

Leo *begins reading the folder of papers.*

Sheena   I feel like the Queen visiting the shipyards.

Martin   What about me?

Leo   What?

Martin   I don't have a hat now.

Leo   Just get the phone.

Sheena   I won't be a minute. The meter's running. Is that your son?

Martin   Do you want me to answer?

Leo   He helps me.

Sheena   Are you a builder as well?

Leo   Architect.

Martin   Bicycle courier.

Sheena   Well. Pleased to meet you . . .

Martin   Martin.
Do you still want me to get the phone?

Leo   Yes.

Sheena   Like Dean Martin.

Martin   What?

Sheena   Before your time.

Martin   No.

Leo   I don't follow this, Mrs Mackie.
This petition you've got here.
This correspondence.
It's been sorted out. The council have spoken to me about the Eden Court flats. I've talked to them about it. They're going to refurbish them . . . I've sent designs . . . I don't see what you're getting at.

Martin   Martin Sheen maybe.

Sheena   You didn't know?

Leo   No.

Sheena   I'm not sure how to say this.
The problem is . . . we . . .
I mean, us, the tenants . . . we don't want the flats refurbished.

Martin   Martin Luther King.

Bored, **Martin** *has begun to play with the model, piling buildings on top of each other. Moving them around.*

Leo   But they need work. Some of those blocks haven't been maintained for years . . .

Martin   Martina Navratilova.

Leo   I told the housing executive. They'll fall apart if work isn't done on them soon. The surveyor's report was . . . Martin, don't do that!

Martin   Just curious.

Leo   The problem's under control. The work's being done for you.

Sheena   We don't want the flats done up, Mr Black. We want them knocked down.

Leo   . . .

Sheena   We've got a petition. Signed by every resident. That copy's for you. There's a copy gone to the council, one to the paper and one to Prince Charles. He signed it.

Leo   Christ.

Sheena   Well, he's interested in that sort of thing, isn't he? Buildings. He's concerned. Not professionally but like an ordinary person. Isn't he?

Leo   He's not an architect. No.

Sheena   Mr Black, we just want houses. We've been in Eden Court, some of us, for twenty years . . .
This isn't a new problem. We've tried but things have gone too far now. We're not interested in plastering over the cracks any more. We want to live in proper houses, decently built.

Leo   I see.

Sheena   It's nothing personal.

Leo   Of course.

Sheena   No offence.

Leo   None taken.

Sheena   You'll consider the petition then?

Leo   I don't really see how I can help you.

Sheena   You can give us your support.

Leo   To demolish my own buildings?

Sheena   Our flats.

Leo   My design.

Martin   You could bomb them.

Leo   I don't see why you need my signature.
I'd have thought there was plenty people who wanted to see
the back of Eden Court.

Martin   From the sky. Planes.

Leo   People in this country don't like anything unless it's
thatched.

Martin   Smart bombs.

Sheena   The council don't want to build a new estate.
They say there isn't the money. It's cheaper to slap a bit of
paint on and leave the place to fall apart. We could take
them to court but something like this could take years. The
only way we'll get what we want is if we embarrass the
council. And if you say they need to be rebuilt they'll have to
do something. They can hardly argue with the architect, can
they?

Leo   Or Prince Charles.
. . .
You're very well organised, Mrs Mackie. This is . . . it's
impressive.

Sheena   Thank you.

Leo   You've put a lot of work into it.

Sheena   We have.

Leo   There's obviously . . . a lot of strong feeling in what
you say.

Sheena   Obviously.

Leo   But the feelings are misdirected, I'm afraid.
The Eden Court flats are good buildings.
Technically.

Martin   What's wrong with them.

Sheena   They're cold, the lifts don't work . . .

Leo   There's nothing wrong with the design.

Martin   Is that all?

Sheena   Most of the flats are infested with cockroaches.

Leo   There wasn't enough money spent on them at the time . . .

Martin   Get Rentokil.

Leo   But if the council are prepared to spend the money now I don't see the need for destruction.

Sheena   They're a new breed of cockroach. A new mutation. There's been a documentary.

Leo   If you look at my proposals . . .

Sheena   They can't be killed in the ordinary way.

Leo   I realise that, I understand there's a depth of emotion. Tower blocks do cause . . . passion. I know that. But if I could . . . persuade you about this . . . I don't think there needs to be . . .

Sheena   We're not asking you to say sorry or anything, Mr Black. We just want you to consider the petition. These signatures. That's the people that live in Eden Court . . .

Leo   But destruction . . .

Sheena   People get things wrong . . . that's fair enough.

Leo   These are understandable grievances but . . .

Sheena   You've got a chance to help fix it.

Leo   Individual problems like this can be solved.

Sheena   You've got a chance to make things right.

Leo   You can't just blow something up for no reason . . . You can't just destroy something that's perfectly sound . . .

Sheena   Look, Mr Black. The taxi's waiting. Now that we've met. Actually made contact. Maybe I could arrange an appointment. Talk to you once you've read everything.

Leo   I won't change my mind. I'm sorry.

Sheena   You know, it's funny to think it was you that built them.

Leo Is it?

Sheena Not you in particular. I just mean it's funny to
think someone thought them up. You know, a person. You
always feel as though they just happened. You're not
insulted, are you?

Leo I assure you . . .

Sheena It's just . . . seeing you. Face to face, I mean. It's
funny.
Well. I'll be in touch. (*To* **Martin**.) Nice to have met you.

Sheena *leaves.* **Martin** *considers the model. Now considerably
rearranged.*

Leo Jesus Christ.

Martin Boom.

Leo What?

Martin Boom.

Lights down.

3

Later. A suburban garden. **Dorothy** *is sitting on a deckchair wearing
a short summer dress and sunglasses. A radio is playing quietly beside
her. On a table in the garden is a pile of delicate sandwiches and a jug of
lemonade.* **Paulina** *is examining her plants. She is overdressed for the
sun and wearing gardening gloves. She touches a plant.*

Paulina Black. See? Half an inch of black poison on the
stem. You should cover up. That's just what's hanging in the
air. It's worse in the sunshine. Some sort of chemical reaction
takes place with the sun, makes it worse, apparently. You
should cover up. You'll burn. If that's what's hanging in the
air, imagine what's settling in your lungs and blood and
everything. Illnesses are up. Cancers are up. Sicknesses are
up. Dorothy? Are you listening to me. You'll burn alive
under that sun. Dorothy?

She smells a rose.

No scent. Proof. If proof were needed. The scent's been poisoned out of them. They only look like flowers now. You have to ask yourself what next. I saw a cyclist stop at the lights. Imagine cycling, in this city, you could be dragged off and beaten at any junction. He was wearing a surgeon's mask. It was black. The gauze was black as tar. Like a swab soaked in black blood. That's just what's in the air.

An aeroplane passes loudly overhead.

Dorothy.
Dorothy.
Dorothy!

The noise has quietened. The radio still plays.

You should cover up. You should cover up before whatever's going to fall from the sky falls from the sky and gets on to your skin. Your father'll be back soon.

. . .

She makes her way indoors.

. . . You won't tan, you know. You don't tan. You'll burn. Look like a bad tomato. You should put some proper clothes on.

Paulina *exits. The radio continues to play.* **Dorothy** *hitches her skirt up her legs a little and rubs oil into them. She relaxes back in the deckchair. After some moments* **Leo** *enters. He is hot. He walks in front of* **Dorothy** *towards the house. He can't help but look at his daughter. He stands by the sandwich table and agonisingly stares, looks away, stares.*

Leo Sandwiches.

Dorothy Dad.

She pulls her skirt down.

Leo They look . . . delicious.

Dorothy Have one. They're for you.

Leo I'll just . . .

Leo takes a sandwich. He leaves. **Martin** *has been watching. He waits till* **Leo** *is indoors. He goes over to the table and picks up a sandwich. He stares at* **Dorothy**. *He goes over to her and lifts her skirt.*

Martin   Nice cunt.

Dorothy *stops him.*

Dorothy   Don't.

Martin   Shame you're wearing pants.

Dorothy   Martin.

Martin   You don't think of your sister having a cunt, do you? Barbie-smooth, you imagine. Surprising.

Dorothy   Stop it.

Martin   Nice though. If that's what you like. Let him have a good look, did you?

Dorothy   He wasn't looking.

Martin   I just saw him.

Dorothy   Leave it, Martin.

Martin   It's understandable I suppose, at his age, no harm in a look.

Dorothy   Don't say that.

Martin   I can see the attraction. You sat there. So secretarial. So available.

Dorothy   What does that mean?

Martin   Does he do it at work? When you take dictation?

Dorothy   You've got a warped mind.

Martin   To think I sprang from his loins. Made of the same stuff. The scientists are baffled.

Dorothy   Please.

Martin *(taking another sandwich)*   Did you make these?

Dorothy   Yes.

Martin   I'm going to be a chef. I've been thinking about it.
In France. I'll get taught. It's an admired art in France you
know. Cuisine. Means kitchen and cooking. Same word. I
think I might be a bastard.

Dorothy   You are.

Martin   No, really. An actual bastard. I think mum fucked
someone else. I'm not like him, am I? Do you think I'm like
him?

Dorothy   Yes.

Martin   No, I'm not. I'm like mum.

Dorothy   Why do you have to say such horrible things
about him?
Why do you have to attack him?

Martin   I'm not attacking him.

Dorothy   You are. He thinks you avoid him.

Martin   I do.

Dorothy   He notices. He gets hurt. He wants this to work.

Martin   Dorothy, I came home because I ran out of
money.
No other reason.
A business arrangement.
. . .
Does that shock you?

Dorothy   If you just try, Martin.

Martin   It shocks me.

Leo *enters. He is carrying a deckchair and a whisky.*

Leo   Thought I'd take the sun.
Catch the last of it.
Lovely sandwiches.

Martin   I made them.

Leo   Did you?

Dorothy   I made them.

Leo   Still . . .

Martin   Have one.

Leo   No. I'm . . . not for me.

Martin   You said they were lovely.

Leo   Yes, they are. I mean. I meant they look lovely. Well done.

Martin   I'm thinking of setting up a sandwich bar.

Dorothy   Martin.

Martin   These are a sort of trial run. A place in the West End. Don't you think?

Dorothy   He's joking.

Martin   Sandwiches for offices, for people just passing by, someone's shopping, they're a bit peckish, they might fancy a sandwich. A BLT . . .

Dorothy   I made them.

Martin   B for bacon, L for lettuce and T for tomato. It's American.

Dorothy   He knows that.

Martin   The classic sandwich. Go on. Try one.

Leo   No. Thank you.

Martin   It's a good idea though, isn't it? Gap in the market.

Leo   It's not a good idea, Martin, it's rubbish. Can we please stop talking about this? It's a perfect afternoon. I don't want to argue on a perfect afternoon.

Martin   Who's arguing? What's the argument?

Dorothy   Stop it.

Leo   Why don't we just . . . enjoy the sun together? Martin, get yourself a chair, why don't you have a drink?

Leo *strips to the waist and settles into the deckchair. He closes his eyes.*
Dorothy *clutches herself suddenly, as though a wave of nausea has passed over her.*

Martin   Don't.
Don't do that.
It doesn't make any difference when you do that.
You always do that.
It's your oldest trick.

Leo's *eyes are open although neither* **Dorothy** *nor* **Martin** *notice.*

Dorothy   I'm not ... doing. I just ...

Martin   I said it didn't make any difference.

Dorothy   Martin.

She reaches for him as she recovers. She tries to steady herself.

Martin   Look at you.

Martin *leaves.*

Leo   Are you all right?

Dorothy   What?
. . .
Oh. Me? Fine. Yes. Just a bit ... You know. Indigestion.
That's all.

Leo   I shouldn't have shouted at him, I just get, when he
babbles like that I get ...
. . .
I offered him the job, you know.

Dorothy   He told me.

Leo   I think he's interested.

Dorothy   We were talking about it just now.

Leo   What did he say?

Dorothy   He said he thought it was good ... a good idea.

Leo   He likes the idea?

Dorothy   He said he thought it was, an interesting business arrangement.

Leo   He would be good at it, you know, he doesn't think so but he could do it . . . He only needs to . . . get to grips with himself. He's still drifting but if I can . . . now that he's come home if we can bring him in . . . give him some . . . solidity. He said he used to play with the models. When he was little. I'd forgotten that . . .

Dorothy   We could all work together.

Leo   No more big projects. That's what I said to him. I'm tired of big projects . . . they run away from you. We'll stay small . . . keep everything under control.
Do you enjoy working for me, Dorothy?

Dorothy   What do you mean?

Leo   Do you like it?

Dorothy   I love it. I mean. It's fine. It's good.

Leo   You do the mail, don't you?

Dorothy   Mostly. Why?

Leo   And my calls. Do you answer the phone usually or does Sylvia?

Dorothy   Have I done something wrong?

Leo   I'm just asking.

Dorothy   If there's a mistake I'll . . .

Leo   There's no mistake.
I was just asking . . . just thinking.

Dorothy   Tell me.

Leo   I don't know what I'd do without you. That's all.
I was just thinking.
I don't know what I'd do without you.

Lights down.

4

Darkness. The quiet dripping sound of a gents public toilet. **Martin** *stands at a urinal with an empty Jenners' bag next to him . . .*

5

The roar of motorway traffic. **Dorothy** *standing beside a motorway at night. Her thumb out for a lift. Cars and lorries thunder past.*

6

Leo *and* **Paulina** *in their bedroom.* **Paulina** *looking in the mirror.*

Leo   He said he was interested . . . He seems . . . when he talks sense . . . I think we're making progress . . . Paulina?

Paulina   Hmm?

Leo   You've been sitting there for half an hour.

Paulina   I'm looking at my face.
It's changed.

Leo   It doesn't change when you look at it. It changes when you look away. Get dressed. We need to go . . .

Paulina   Leo. I don't want to go.

Leo   What?

Paulina   I never said I wanted to go.

Leo   I've bought tickets . . . There's people expecting us.

Paulina   I've heard it's terrible.
Makes no sense apparently.
Apparently it's the product of a diseased imagination.
I don't want to wallow in it.

Leo   We sponsored it.
It's supposed to be important.
It's a state of the nation play.

Paulina   I don't like tragedy.

Leo   It's farce.

Paulina   You go. If you want to go.

Leo   It's colleagues and wives. It's a colleagues and wives thing. I can't go alone.

Paulina   Stay then.

Leo   What do you want me to do? Do you want me to stay?

Paulina   Do you notice anything about the bedroom, Leo?

Leo   I'll stay if you want me to stay.

Paulina   A bed. Walls. Bedside table. Perfume. Face cream. Can you smell anything?

Leo   I can't say I noticed.

Paulina   No. You don't notice it until you notice it. Then you can't get rid of it.

Leo   I'll stay. I'll ring them and say you're ill.

7

The side of a motorway. The noise of traffic. **Dorothy** *hitching. A lorry pulls up. Its headlights flood the stage. Blinding.* **Dorothy** *gets into the lorry.*

8

The sound of dripping water. The inside of a public toilet. **Martin** *is still standing at the urinal.* **Billy** *enters. He stands near* **Martin** *at the urinal. They move together. Suddenly* **Billy** *kneels.* **Martin** *holds his head.*

9

Dorothy *and* **Joe** *in the cab of* **Joe**'s *lorry.*

Dorothy   Sometimes I want to run at the side of a house.
I get the feeling.
A red-bricked gable end.
Just turn and run at it straight. Full speed, as though it
wasn't there. Smack it and feel the bricks cut me.
Feel my skull smack.
Slide down half conscious.
Pick myself up and do it again.

Joe   Any particular house?

Dorothy   Mine. Anyone's. It doesn't matter so long as it's
made of bricks. I don't even need to be near a house to get the
feeling. I could be anywhere. At a party, in the office, in a
field and suddenly I want to smash myself against an outside
wall.

Joe   I get feelings like that sometimes.

Dorothy   Really?

Joe   All the time. In the lorry, on the motorway, now even.
I could just yank the steering wheel and twist off the road.
Plough into a bus full of schoolchildren and not stop.

He turns his hand on the steering wheel.

Just that.

He repeats the movement.

That's all it would take.
It's quite common to feel that, among lorry drivers.

Dorothy   Something stops you though?

Joe   Not much. The skin of the milk. Not much more than
that. There was a lorry driver once. It was famous. He was
driving his lorry across the Sahara Desert and he crashed . . .
right into a tree.

Dorothy   I thought there weren't any trees in the Sahara
Desert.

Joe   Only one. That's the point of the story. He crashes into
the most isolated tree in the world. Nothing but emptiness

and sand for thousands of miles in any direction and there's
this tree and he hits it. Killed himself. Killed the tree. People
said it was insanity or coincidence or fate but I can
understand it. In the middle of the desert you see a tree, one
tree and ...

He repeats the movement.

... you drive at it.
Of course you do.

Dorothy   You shouldn't be allowed on the road.

Joe   All drivers get it. Coach drivers particularly. You
wouldn't become a coach driver unless you were fascinated
by death. It's all they talk about. Still. I don't want to worry
you. Touch wood.

*He touches **Dorothy**'s leg, momentarily.*

How far are you going?

Dorothy   As far as you're going. Somewhere far away. As
far away as possible.

Joe   Hull. And back.

Dorothy   Hull then.

10

*The gents toilet. In a cubicle. **Billy** is standing inside the Jenners'
bag, his face turned against the wall. **Martin** is behind him with his
hands between his legs. **Billy** turns round to kiss **Martin**.*

Martin   No.

Billy   Go on.

Martin   No.

Martin *almost pushes **Billy** away.*

11

Leo *eating.* **Paulina** *watching. Silence.*

Leo   This is nice.

Paulina   Do you think so?

Leo   Really.
Good.
Home cooking.

Paulina   I bought it.

Leo   Shame the kids . . .
Seems silly to call them kids . . .
Doesn't seem the right word, does it?
Shame they couldn't eat with us.
We should eat together more. As a family.
If I'd known we . . . I'd have asked . . .

Paulina   They're out. Didn't say where.

Leo   A family dinner. Now Martin's home. Everyone
round the table. Do the washing up together . . . like we used
to.

Paulina   Shut your mouth, Leo.

Leo   What?

Paulina   When you're eating. Shut your mouth.

Leo   Sorry.

Paulina   You always do it.
Have you noticed that?
You don't think I need to see what's in your mouth. I cooked
it. I don't need a display.

Leo   It's delicious. Very well made. It should be on display.
Why don't you have some wine?

Paulina   No.

Leo *pours himself a glass.*

Leo   You remember Eden Court? Paulina?
The housing estate I did . . . for the council . . .
'71 I think, feels like yesterday of course,
Martin was just born.

A woman came to me today.
She wants it blown up.

Paulina   Are you having an affair?

Leo   ...
I'm sorry?

Paulina   Have you had one? Recently?

Leo   What makes you think ...

Paulina   I'm asking.

Leo   No. No. I haven't, Paulina. No.
...
I'm not having an affair.

Paulina   You wouldn't tell me if you were.

Leo   Is there some kind of problem here, you don't believe
me?

Paulina   You were chatting. You usually chat to me when
you feel guilty about something.

Leo   For God's sake. I was talking about work.

Paulina   I don't know how you can drink that.

Leo   I said they want to demolish Eden Court.

Paulina   They tread on them. The grapes.

Leo   A thing I built. They want to destroy it.

Paulina   There's probably sweat in it.

Leo   I thought you'd want to know. That's all.

Paulina   Foot diseases and whatever else.

Leo   It's traditional. Traditionally that's how they make
wine.

Paulina   It turns my stomach.

Leo   It's a typical attitude, of course. Blame the architect.
People are poor. Blame the architect. Place is a slum, blame
the architect. They fill a place with pigs and then complain
it's turned into a pigsty.

Paulina   They probably urinate, the treaders, for revenge.

Leo   What?

Paulina   Revenge. They probably laugh as it runs down their legs.

Leo   I don't think so.

Paulina   You don't know what goes on in a person's mind.

Leo   It's good wine.

Paulina   All sorts of thoughts.

Leo   I thought you liked claret.

Paulina   Shut your mouth, Leo, you're doing it again . . .

Leo   I never understand the point of table manners you know. Fork this side, fork that side. It's all class. There's no beauty in it. No truth. Do you know, in some countries, if you're enjoying a meal, it's considered polite to belch. When I was in Saudi . . .

Paulina   If you want to belch go into the garden.

Leo   I don't want to belch, I'm just saying . . .

Paulina   Make your noises there.

Leo   I'm making a point. Table manners aren't . . .

Paulina   Excuse me.

Paulina *gets up and leaves.*

Leo   Paulina!
Paulina.

. . .

He pours another glass. Lights a cigarette.

12

Billy *and* **Martin** *in the streets.* **Billy** *walks behind* **Martin**. **Martin** *is trying to shake him off.*

Billy   Mister. Oi. Mister. Wait.

Martin   ...

Billy *catches up with him.*

Billy   Billy.

Martin   What d'you want?

Billy   What's your name.

Martin   None of your fucking business.

Billy   Just asking.

Martin   If I'd wanted you to know my name I'd tell you it.
Wouldn't I?

Billy   I know but ...

Martin   So stop following me.

Billy   I've never seen you there before.
You're new.
Usually old blokes ...

Martin *begins to move off.* **Billy** *follows him.*

Billy   Married ... pot bellies and smelly dicks.
You're not married, are you ...

Martin   I told you to fucking stop.

Billy *points to a shop window. In the shop window is a green jacket on a stand.*

Billy   Have you seen this jacket.

Martin   You keep talking to me.

Billy   It's like that jacket. You know, the one John Wayne
wore in *The Quiet Man.*

Martin   Stop it.

Billy   You'd suit green, you'd look good in it.

Martin   I'm going to walk away. If you follow me I'm
going to run. If you keep following me I'm going to punch
you.

Billy   D'you promise?

Martin   I'll hit your face and I'll keep hitting it until you
leave me alone. You don't want that, do you?

Billy   Are you rich? You look quite rich. Are you?

Martin   . . .

Billy   Your accent. You could probably buy that jacket. As
a present to yourself.

Martin   I warned you . . .

Martin *approaches* **Billy** *as if about to hit him.* **Billy** *suddenly
turns and punches through the glass of the shop window.*

13

Paulina *and* **Leo**. *The phone rings.* **Paulina** *has returned.*

Leo   No comment.
No comment.
I'm sorry.
I've told you no comment.
The buildings are structurally sound.
That's all I'm prepared to say at the moment.
No comment.
Thank you.
Goodbye.
Fucking idiot.
. . .
Newspaper.
You should eat something.

Paulina   No.

Leo   You're making yourself ill.

Paulina   Just the thought of it. I can't.

Leo   It's a chicken, Paulina, just chicken.

Paulina   I saw a programme about it.

Leo   Perfectly good food.

Paulina   Probably riddled with disease.

Leo   It looks fine to me. You cooked it.

Paulina   If you had an affair you wouldn't tell me, would you?

Leo *puts some food on a plate and pushes it towards her.*

Paulina   No.

Leo   You're not turning vegetarian on me, are you?

Paulina   Maybe. Maybe I'll stop eating altogether.

Leo   I'm not having an affair, Paulina. Now eat something.

Paulina   Fruit. I'll be fruitarian.

Leo   Jesus.

Paulina   I couldn't plan for it. If you had an affair. I wouldn't know until it had happened.

Leo   It won't happen.

Paulina   You'd disguise your guilt by paying me more attention.

Leo   Don't be stupid.

Paulina   You could infect me. I wouldn't know. I couldn't plan for it.

Leo   Christ, Paulina, you're like a needle picking at a splinter. Jab jab jab. We're having dinner. I don't need this kind of . . . this . . . whatever it is you're trying to prove . . . Can't you just . . . Make small talk, be normal, eat the chicken, for God's sake . . .

Paulina   The thought of bird flesh. Rotting inside me.

Leo   Why did you cook it then?
Why did you cook the fucking thing if you didn't want to eat it?

Paulina   Habit, probably.
. . .
I'm sorry.

Pause. **Paulina**, *still, quietly, begins to weep.* **Leo** *goes to her, stands behind her and holds her.*

Leo   Is something wrong? Did I say something? Paulina, what's the matter?

Paulina   Pesticides on fruit.

Leo   Paulina.

Paulina   The rain rains on it. Washes the chemicals off.

Leo   Love.

Paulina   And then the rain's dirty. Full of poison.

Leo *tries to kiss her neck.*

Leo   Please don't cry.

Paulina   Don't leave me, Leo.
Don't go away.

Leo   I'm not going anywhere.

Paulina   They've gone. Don't you go too.

14

A Country Kitchen motorway service station. **Dorothy** *and* **Joe** *are sitting at a table. Their chairs are fixed to the floor. The light is sterile. It is dark outside.* **Joe** *is drinking tea from a jumbo-sized paper cup.* **Dorothy** *has been sleeping.*

Dorothy   What time is it?

Joe   Late. Nearly home. I bought you a tea.

Dorothy   Thank you.

Joe (*sings*)   It's four in the morning and once more the dawning . . .
. . .
Don't you want it?

Dorothy   No. How close are we?

Joe   An hour or so.
It'll get cold. You should drink it.

A nice hot cup of tea.
Do you good. Rinse out the insides.

Dorothy   I don't like tea.

Joe   Everyone likes tea. Except snobs.
You're not a coffee drinker, are you?

Dorothy   I just feel a bit . . .
You know . . . a bit.

Joe   I thought you might be thirsty, that's all.

Dorothy *clutches herself. A wave of nausea passes over her.*

Joe   Are you all right?

Dorothy   Yes.

Joe   You don't seem it.

Dorothy   I'm fine. It's finished now.

Joe   Moaning and groaning.

Dorothy   Honestly. I know what it is. It's gone now.
Honestly.

Joe   Are you sure you don't want some tea?

Dorothy   No.

Joe   It's still warm. They gave me a jumbo cup.
They know me here. I'm a regular.
I always stop and I always have a jumbo.
I don't even have to ask.
The girls just know.
Do your parents know where you are?

Dorothy   No.

Joe   They must be worried.

Dorothy   No.

Joe   I'm sorry. I don't mean to pry. Only I get runaways.
Hitching. You feel responsible.

Dorothy   I just needed to get away. I'm not . . . it's just
something I do from time to time. No one worries.

Joe   If your father got hold of me he'd go mad. Wouldn't he? If he could see us now?

Dorothy   He won't notice.

Joe   You've been away all night.

Dorothy   I'll be back in the morning.
Where are we now?

Joe   Junction 17.

Dorothy   What are we carrying?

Joe   Barbed wire. Sheet metal. Fences. Security gear.

Dorothy   Are we nearly there?

Joe   If you look out that window you can see the lights of the skyscrapers, the tallest ones. See . . . that's forty miles away. Forty miles. Amazing. Would he go mad? Your father?

Dorothy   What's in between?

Joe   What?

Dorothy   Here and there.

Joe   Road.

Dorothy   There must be more than just road.

Joe   Well. Road and . . .
Obviously there's towns.

Dorothy   Which ones?

Joe   Small ones. You know. More suburbs in fact. Suburbs you'd call them.
. . .
And fields I suppose.

Dorothy   What do they grow?

Joe   Cows I think. Mainly. It's cows you see anyway.

Dorothy *wipes her face with a napkin. She examines the napkin.*

Dorothy   How long was I asleep?

Joe   Most of the way. You just curled up on the seat.

Dorothy   I'm sorry.

Joe   Why?

Dorothy   I didn't chat. I slept.

Joe   I drive a truck. I'm used to my own company.
I wouldn't say I enjoy it but I tolerate it.
I'm like an old married couple. I tolerate myself.

Dorothy   It was warm. You had the heater on. I couldn't
keep my eyes open. I always sleep best in trucks.

Joe   Did you dream?

Dorothy   No dreams.

Joe   You looked peaceful. Nice.

Dorothy   I'm sorry I slept. It wasn't what you wanted.

Joe   I enjoyed your presence. That was company enough.
As a matter of fact it's nice to have a girl beside you as you
drive. Do your parents know where you go? When you're on
these trips?

Dorothy   They never ask.

Joe   With a boyfriend?

Dorothy   Probably.

Joe   Don't they want to meet him? Talk to him?

Dorothy   We don't have that in our family.

Joe   What?

Dorothy   Asking. Telling.

Joe   Still.

Dorothy   What do you mean nice?

Joe   ...

Dorothy   Nice to have a girl.

Joe   I didn't mean to offend you. Any man would ... would
feel ...

Dorothy   What?

Joe   It doesn't matter. I shouldn't have said.

Dorothy   Go on.

Joe   Just having a girl near you. Your skin on the seat. Your breathing. That's all.

Dorothy   Tell me.

Joe   You know.

Dorothy   Say.

Joe   Any man would. A girl.

Dorothy   I turned you on?

Joe   No.
Yes.
No. Not 'turned on'. That's not the right words.

Dorothy   What then.

Joe   Moved. I was moved.

Dorothy   In what way?

Joe   Powerfully.

Dorothy   Powerfully in what way?

Joe   This is stupid. Just forget I said anything.

Dorothy   I want to know.

Joe   It's a mixture of things . . . a man's feelings . . . they . . . you become sort of . . . full of . . . wanting.

Dorothy   Wanting.

Joe   Please don't take offence.

Dorothy   I won't.

Joe   You want to . . . you know . . . touch her. Hold her breasts in your . . . see her . . . you know.

Dorothy   Oh.

Joe   But then I felt something different.

Dorothy   What?

Joe   Sadness. I felt sad for you.

Dorothy   And . . .

Joe   Then I felt sad for me.

Dorothy   And.

Joe   Then I felt sad for us. For everybody.
Funny, isn't it?
. . .
I wanted to hold you.

Dorothy   Why?

Joe   I wanted to protect you. From men like me.

Dorothy   Is that all?

Joe   You're not revolted?

Dorothy   No.

Joe   You don't mind me saying things like this?

Dorothy   It's what I want.

Joe   My wife would never let me say things like this to her.

Dorothy   You could tell her.

Joe   You don't want your wife to know you have these
thoughts. This. Me. Here. You. My heart thumping like this.
A young woman. I couldn't stand it if she knew these things
about me. Looking at girls. Looking at you. I mean. I love
my wife.

Dorothy   Do you?

Joe   Not love exactly. Care. No. It's hard to know the
word. There's a connection between a man and his wife. You
can't break it. Sometimes I think she knows what's
disgusting about me. You think she can read your mind.
Horrible. But you never say anything. You just couldn't.
. . .
We should stop. Talking about this stuff.

Dorothy   We can stop if you want to.
Do you want to?

Joe   No. It's all right.
. . .
Ask more.

Dorothy   Do you look at your wife? When she's asleep?

Joe   I used to but . . . your wife . . . it would be like looking at
your mother.

Dorothy   Did you do anything else? Apart from look at
me?

Joe   No.
Not really.

Dorothy   Say.

Joe   I didn't do anything.

Dorothy   You said . . .

Joe   I tried to touch you. I reached out my hand to . . .
Lift your . . .
But I didn't. I could feel you breathing on my fingertips.
Common decency to stop. Or fear. Skin of the milk. I wanted
to. Nearly fainted from it.
Why do you want to know all this?

Dorothy   Why do you want to tell me?

15

The urgent sound of an alarm. **Billy** *and* **Martin** *on the street by the
smashed shop window.* **Billy** *is holding the green jacket. His hand is
bleeding.*

Billy   For you.

Martin   You smashed it.

Billy   Put it on.

Martin   Put your fist through a fucking window. Jesus.

Billy   Put it on. Go on. It's a present.

Martin   Wait. Billy . . .

Billy   You said Billy.

Martin   I don't want presents. I don't want to know who you are. All I want is for you to go away. You go that way and I'll go this way. Please.

Billy   Made a brilliant noise. Didn't it? Crash.

Martin   You shouldn't have done it.

Billy   Take it. Take the jacket. It's yours.

Martin   I don't want it. You have it.

Billy   I chose it for you.

Martin *takes the jacket.* **Billy** *sits down on the pavement.*

Martin   Thank you.

Billy   Wear it.

Martin   Your hand.

Billy   Wear it.

Martin   You're cut.

Billy   It's a beautiful jacket. Wear it.

Martin *puts the jacket on.*

Billy   Give us a twirl.

Martin   Can you run? You run that way. Let's just run. We'll leave the jacket and run.

Billy *is sitting by the smashed window. His hand is bleeding.* **Martin** *tears a strip off the bottom of his shirt and gives it to* **Billy***.*

Martin   Wrap that round your hand.

Billy   What's this? Guess this? (*American accent.*) For a minute there I thought we were in trouble.

Martin   I don't want to know.

Billy (*American accent*)   For a minute there I thought we . . .

Martin   Please. I'm asking. Run.

Billy   Can you guess it?

Martin   Will you run, you mad cunt?

Billy   Right. We're surrounded, by hundreds and hundreds of Mexican police, you're bandaging my hand . . . Can you guess it . . . ?

Martin   Why are you doing this?

Billy (*American*)   Wait a minute. Did you hear something?

Martin   Where?

Billy   No. It's part of the film. You have to guess.

Martin   Billy.

Billy (*American*)   For a minute there I thought we were in trouble.

Billy *enacts the final moment from* Butch Cassidy and the Sundance Kid. *He stands up, ready to spring into action, guns blazing and just as he comes out of the imaginary building he freezes and makes the sound of thousands of guns going off.*

Martin *puts his hand over* **Billy**'s *mouth. Eventually lets go of him.*

Billy   *Butch Cassidy and the Sundance Kid.*
Final scene. I videoed it off the telly.
That looks a bit tight around the arms, you know.
Do you want a size larger?

Martin   All right. You win. I know a place. We'll go there. Let's just get out of here before the police come.

Billy   Where? Your place?

Martin   Just a place I know. Near here. I go sometimes. Come on.

Billy *is looking at his reflection in what remains of the shop window.*

Billy   Look at us. You be Sundance. I'll be Butch.

Martin   Let's just go.

Billy (*American*)   Whaddaya mean you can't swim? The fall'll probably kill ya.

Martin   Hurry up.

Billy *takes* **Martin**'s *hand. Pretends to jump off a cliff.*

Billy   Whoooooooaaaaaaah.

Looking at their reflection **Billy** *kisses* **Martin** *sexually.*

Martin   Billy.
Billy.
What are you doing?
Don't.

He pushes **Billy** *off him.*

What the fuck do you think I am?
Christ.

16

Leo *and* **Paulina**. *A dim light.* **Paulina** *is clearing up dinner plates and wiping.*

Leo   When we were first together.

She wipes around him.

I thought you were the most beautiful thing I'd ever seen.

Paulina   Are you finished?

Leo   Oh. Yes. Thank you.
Everything about you was perfect and I made sure to keep you. I thought about you all the time. About how things would be? About what I'd do . . .

She goes into the kitchen. **Leo** *lights a cigarette.*

But you start with things, you draw up plans and then they get confused. People spoil things and . . . time and you lose the clarity. So you have to get back to the original . . . go back to the drawing board . . .

. . .

We'll get out of the city. Paulina. A village somewhere. We'll do up a house or something. I'll work from the attic. Get back to the original us ... all of us ... You, me, Dorothy, Martin ...

Paulina You're smoking.

Leo You know, Paulina, you're still a lovely looking woman.

Paulina Put it out.

Leo For your age. Considering. You are.

Paulina I said you weren't to smoke here.

Leo I want to smoke. It's a lovely night. I've had a lovely meal. Stars in a black sky and this is my lovely wife.

Paulina *takes the cigarette from his hand and stubs it out.*

Leo I look at you sometimes and I think, I can see you when you were twenty-two ... when I first ...

Paulina You said you wouldn't do that.

Leo I can see the original, and I think ... I want to say ...

Paulina Not in the house. I asked you.

Leo I know you don't like me saying it but ...

Paulina Fumes and ...

Leo It doesn't stop me from wanting to say it.

Paulina Dirt and ...

Leo I look at you and I want to say ...
You're a beautiful woman.

Paulina Ashes and ...

Leo It's pleasant just to sit here and look at you.

Paulina Stop it, Leo.

Leo I mean it.

Paulina Stop.

Leo   I want to say it. I feel it.
It's objectively true.
You're beautiful.

Paulina   Leo.

Leo   My beautiful wife.

Paulina *throws a plate down onto the floor, it breaks.*

Leo   Paulina!

Paulina   Don't call me that.

Leo   Well, what do you want me to call you then?

Paulina   At the moment, nothing.

Leo   I have to call you something. I can't just point at you.

Paulina   I don't want you to refer to me.

. . .

Leo   I'm sorry. I should have offered to help with the clearing up.

. . .

Paulina, what's wrong?

Paulina   I said not to smoke.

Leo   I know, love, but after a meal, I like to . . .

Paulina   Why did I do that?

Leo   You were upset. It's understandable. I'm sorry.

Paulina   Plate throwing. It's so . . . domestic.

Leo   I'll clear it up. You sit down.

Paulina   So banal.

Leo, *on his hands and knees starts to pick up pieces of plate.* **Paulina** *sits.*

Leo   You snapped. That's all. What with Martin coming home and . . . I've not been in the best of moods. I've not helped. You snapped. It's probably a good thing.

Paulina   Such a poor gesture.

Leo   The thing is . . . we need to get things clear between us.
I've let you drift away from me. We don't communicate. The
two of us. In our own worlds. But we're lucky. That's what
we have to remember. We're the lucky ones. We have
everything . . . that's what's important to remember.

*He is now standing behind her. He tries to kiss her. Her resistance is
tired.*

You feel so good.

Paulina   Leo.

Leo   So soft.

Paulina   Go to bed.

Leo   So lovely.

*He starts trying to undress her. She is stiff. Corpse-like, she gives
nothing. He continues. He kisses her breasts. She holds his head. She
tolerates him.*

So lovely. Such a beautiful woman. So beautiful.

17

Joe and **Dorothy** *in the motorway service station.*

Joe   I've got a confession to make.

Dorothy   Go on.

Joe   In the cab. I was listening to country music. Do you
like country music?

Dorothy   I don't know.

Joe   Marty Robbins? Do you know Marty Robbins? El
Paso? Devil Woman? White Sport Coat?
(*Sings.*) 'A white sport coat, and a pink carnation . . . I'm all
dressed up, for the dance.'

Dorothy   Is that your confession?

Joe   I was listening to the song and . . .

. . .

I touched myself.
I didn't touch you.
One hand was reaching over to touch you but with the other I unzipped and . . .

Dorothy   Who was driving the lorry for God's sake?

Joe   We were stopped. Out there, in the lorry park. I couldn't bear to wake you up.
. . .
Are you sure you don't want some tea?

Dorothy   Sure.

Joe   You could have me arrested.

Dorothy   Could I?

Joe   Sent to prison.

Dorothy   I've only got your word for it. I didn't see anything.

Joe   But I confessed.

Dorothy   People confess all the time. It means nothing. Hardened criminals confess to cover their tracks.

Joe   Do you feel violated?

Dorothy   Do you want me to?

Joe   . . .
Yes.

Dorothy *doubles up again, holding herself as before.*

Joe   What's wrong?

Dorothy   I get attacks. It's nothing.

Joe   Attacks? Attacks of what?

Dorothy   Dread. Don't laugh at me.

Joe   I'd never.

Dorothy   I get signals. Messages. Warnings. I'm not mental.

Joe   Of course you're not.

Dorothy   Can we leave?

Joe   It could be . . . you know . . . woman-related. You've
all sorts of organs down there. It could be any one of them.

Dorothy   Let's go to the lorry. Please.

Joe   These signals. Do you know where they come from?

Dorothy   No.

Joe   Maybe it's my fault.

Dorothy   No.

Joe   Maybe I'm signalling you. Maybe that's what you've
been receiving. I felt something. All night maybe I've been
sending out signals. Like dolphin calls across the ocean floor.
Perhaps it's something like that . . .

He demonstrates.

Poooooooooooow . . . Poooooooooooooow . . .
Poooooooooooow

Dorothy *laughs.*

Dorothy   Must be different frequencies, Joe. It's not your
signals I'm getting. Your signals must be being picked up
somewhere else.

18

Billy *and* **Martin** *on the roof of a tall building. Night.* **Billy** *is
tuning a small radio. He moves around the roof searching for a signal.*
Martin *is sitting on the edge of the roof, his legs dangling into space.
Below, there is a carpet of lights stretching into the far distance. The
sounds of the city float up from below, less like real noises than like
memories of noises.*

The radio picks up crackles and whines, snatches of music. Eventually
Billy *settles on a signal. A pop song. He loses it and changes position.
He gains the signal again by balancing on the edge of the roof.
Precariously. We hear the first bars of 'Take Me Home Country
Roads' by John Denver.* **Billy** *is absolutely still . . .*

Billy   Listen.

Martin   Shhh.

Billy   Listen.

Martin   Shhh.

Billy   Martin...

Martin   Billy.

19

A garden in the suburbs. The wind blowing gently. Suddenly
Paulina *enters in some distress. She gags, holding her hand over her
mouth. She goes further into the garden. She vomits.*

20

The roof with **Billy** *and* **Martin**, *as before.*

Billy   Almost heaven...

Martin *tries to keep his composure.*

Billy   West Virginia.

Martin   Billy.

Billy   Blue Ridge Mountains.

Martin   Don't sing.

Billy   Shenandoah River.

Martin   I said, don't sing.

Billy   Life is old there.

Martin   Please.

Billy   Older than the trees.

Martin   Switch it off.

Billy   Younger than the mountains.

Martin   I come here for quiet.

Billy   Growing in the breeze.

Martin *tries to snatch the radio,* **Billy** *holds it out over the edge.*

Billy   Take me home.

Martin   It's supposed to be quiet.

Billy   Country roads.

Martin   You're spoiling it.

Billy   To the place.

Martin   Billy!

Billy   That I belong.

Martin   You're spoiling everything.

Billy   West Virginia.

Martin   Give me that fucking thing.

Billy   Mountain momma.

Martin   I'm warning you.

Billy   Take me home.

Martin *punches* **Billy** *hard.*

Billy   Fuck.

Billy *totters on the edge.* **Martin** *catches him. The radio falls.*

21

The garden. **Paulina** *stands in darkness, recovering.* **Leo** *enters.*

Leo   Paulina.
Where are you?
Are you there?
Paulina.
Paulina.

22

The back of a container lorry. **Dorothy** *and* **Joe** *in a half light, surrounded by barbed wire and security equipment.*

Dorothy   It's cold.

Joe   I'm sorry.

Dorothy   Isn't there any heating?

Joe   In the cab. This is just the container.

Dorothy   What's all this stuff?

Joe   Deliveries.

Dorothy   Barbed wire?

Joe   For building sites. Stops vandals. Kids'll nick anything these days. If it's not nailed down.

Dorothy   Joe...

Joe   If you don't want to...

Dorothy   I don't know.

Joe   We don't have to. We can go.

Dorothy   Kiss me.

Joe   Are you sure?

Dorothy   No.

Joe *approaches her. Cautiously he touches her face.*

Dorothy   Do you want me? Really?

Joe   Yes.

Dorothy   Say it.

Joe   I want you.

Dorothy   Don't touch me.

Joe   But... you said to...

Dorothy   Stand back. Stand there.

Joe   I'm sorry... I didn't mean to upset you...

Dorothy   Look at me.

A pause.

Dorothy   Do you think I'm available?

Joe   I shouldn't have asked you to do this.

Dorothy   It's an important question, Joe. Do you think I'm available?

Joe   No. Of course not.

Dorothy   It's important. Available, Joe.

Joe   . . . Yes. I don't know.

Dorothy   Look at me. What is it about me? What gives you feelings? Tell me.

Joe   This is wrong, Dorothy. This isn't working. You said you wanted . . . My wife . . .

Dorothy   Is it the clothes?

She starts to take off her dress.

Joe   Please don't.

It's cold. She holds herself awkwardly.

Dorothy   Say you want me.

Joe   I want you.

Dorothy   Say I'm yours.

Joe   You're mine.

Dorothy   What does it feel like?

Joe   Dorothy.

Dorothy   Important, Joe. What does it feel like?

Joe   I . . . you're . . . this is embarrassing, Dorothy.

Dorothy   You. Now. Tell me the feeling.

Joe   I feel ashamed. I feel disgusted.

Dorothy   By me?

Joe   This isn't what I imagined. You asked me to come with you. You seemed sure. I didn't mean . . . now you turn round and start this. I thought you . . .
You talked to me, didn't you?
Listened.
You wanted me.
Everything was like a dream come true and now this.
Now you're all . . .
All . . .

Dorothy   What? All what?

Joe   Just get dressed.

Dorothy   Is it my body?

Joe   Please.

Dorothy   Is my body wrong?

Joe   No.

Dorothy   Don't you want to look at it?

Joe   Not like this.

Dorothy   How then? Like this?

She takes up a page-three pose. No smile.

Joe   No!

Dorothy   You have to say. You have to tell me. How do you want me to be? How Joe?

She doubles up again. He approaches her. Holds her. Covers her up. She remains still.

23

Leo *and* **Paulina** *in the garden. Dark.* **Leo** *smoking.* **Paulina** *standing apart.*

Leo   This isn't going to happen, Paulina.

Paulina   I want you to put concrete over the grass.

Leo   I won't lose you.
You have to . . .
We both . . .

Paulina   I don't want grass.

Leo   All of us have to stop this . . . falling apart that's
happening here.

Paulina   I want a patio.

Leo   This is my family.
Families have problems. It's natural. You expect it.

Paulina   Leave a space for the roses.

Leo   But you can't just . . .
You have to pull things back together.

Paulina   All the rest concrete.

24

The roof. **Billy** *and* **Martin**.

Martin   Sorry.

Billy   Been hit worse before.

Martin   You kept going . . . you . . .

Billy   Not even a hit really. A slap it was. Not a punch. I've
had it harder than that.

Martin   I don't hit people. Not normally. Not for pleasure.

Billy   It was all right.

Martin   Don't.

Billy   Motherly, almost.

Martin   For God's sake.

Billy   Warm. Nice.

Martin   I said I was sorry.

Billy   No need.

Martin   I come up here to get away from . . . for silence.
Because it's pure. No voices. No talking.

Billy   I came up for you. I'm the one who should be sorry.

Martin   Twenty floors up you'd think there'd be nothing.
No people, no sound, no signals, no feelings.
And then you.
I had it. Just for a moment.
And then you.

Billy   I spoiled it.

Martin   Blankness. Purity. And then that trash.

Billy   Steady on. I like John Denver.

Martin   That isn't the point.

Billy   I think John Denver is pure.

Martin   Pollution.

Billy   Looks almost like the Milky Bar kid.

Martin   We could have fucked.
We could have.
Us, alone, no mess.
You spoiled it.

Billy   You're upset.

Martin   Yes.

Billy   I thought it was how we were feeling.
I thought it was romantic. Our song.
I've always wanted an 'our song' with someone.
We could have danced.
Like in a film.

Martin   I don't want something that's like in a film.
Something that's like in a film is exactly what I don't want.
I wanted to slip away.

Billy   From what?

Martin   You. Me. Everything.

Billy   If you'd told me.

Martin   It was a perfect moment.

Billy   There'll be another. They probably happen all the time up here. Regular.

Martin   What do you know about perfect moments?

Billy   I know.

Martin   How?

Billy   I just had one then.

25

The inside of the lorry. The engine is turning over. **Dorothy** *and* **Joe** *are parked outside her house.*

Dorothy   I'd better go.

Joe   . . .

Dorothy   I've got work tomorrow.

Joe   . . .

Dorothy   I'm sorry it didn't . . .
I'm sorry I wasn't . . .

Joe   . . .

Dorothy   You weren't to know about me.
I don't know about me.
I'm not nice.
I led you on. Didn't I?

Joe   . . .

Dorothy   Will you see me again? Send signals.
Poooooow . . .
Will you stop for me?

Joe   . . .

Dorothy   Goodbye, Joe.

She kisses his cheek and gets out of the cab.

We see **Paulina** *standing in the garden.*

We see **Leo**.

We see **Billy** *and* **Martin** *standing on the roof.* **Martin** *is standing behind* **Billy** *holding his head.*

Leo   I won't let you drift away, Paulina.

Billy   You can see my house from here.

Leo   We're a good family.

Billy   Martin.
I said you can see . . .

Martin *lets go of* **Billy**'s *head.*

Martin   What makes you think I care where you live?

Leo   I won't let you put up walls between us.

Paulina   You're the architect, Leo.

Billy *suddenly turns and runs full tilt at the edge of the roof.*

Martin   Billy!

Martin *tries to catch him, he has to run full speed after him. They both run towards the edge.*

Blackout.

Act Two

1

Darkness.

Lights suddenly up on **Billy** *being caught by* **Martin** *just as he is about to go over the edge.*

Martin You cunt.

Martin *holds* **Billy***, limply, despairing. In the background we hear a large series of explosions. The sound of applause. Lights down.*

2

Some weeks later.

The garden is in a mess. It has been dug up, ploughed and turned over. There are only scattered patches of green. A pile of concrete paving stones are stacked against the wall of the house. **Leo** *is paving over the garden.*

Paulina *enters carrying plant pots. She begins to transfer plants from the garden into pots. She watches him.*

Leo Working.

Paulina I can see.

Leo It seems a shame to . . .

Paulina It's what I want.

Leo Yes, I know, love, but . . .

Paulina You can sweep patios.

Leo To cover it all though . . .

Paulina Wash them.

Leo It'll take value off the house.
People like a garden.

Paulina I don't want you trailing dirt inside.

Leo But when . . . if we move. When we go to the country . . . it seems a shame.

Paulina Hose yourself down when you're finished.

Martin *comes out. Dressed for going out. He is wearing the green jacket.*

A pause.

Martin You'll kill him.

Paulina Is that what you're wearing?

Martin I've been watching from the bedroom.

Paulina Are you going somewhere?

Martin All that sweating.

Paulina Somewhere you want to attract attention?

Martin Manual labour. He's not used to it. You'll put a strain on his heart.

Paulina You should be careful.

Martin I'm going out.

Paulina Clothes send signals.

Martin He's been at it all afternoon.

Paulina There are people, Martin, who interpret signals. One way or another.

Martin It's a labour of love.

Paulina Signals attract them.

Martin He's moving the earth for you.

Paulina These people.

Martin Is the earth moving for you?

Paulina Even if you don't actually talk to them. They come into your proximity. You should be careful.

Martin You got another spade, boss?

Leo   . . .

Martin   Give us it.

Leo   What for?

Martin   I can just see myself as a digger.

Leo *gives* **Martin** *the spade.* **Martin** *takes his jacket off. They dig together.*

Paulina   I thought you were going out.

Martin   I decided to work instead.

Leo   You could dig there if you want.

Paulina   You'll have to throw away your good clothes.

Martin   Father and son together in honest toil.

Paulina   You'll spoil them.

Martin   Good this, isn't it, boss?

Leo   What?

Martin   Digging.

Paulina   You don't both have to do it.

Martin   You and me. Digging together.

Paulina   It only means two sets of dirt.

Martin   I could dig roads in Canada or something.

Leo   You don't dig roads. You build them.

Martin   Digging's involved though. The company of digging men.

Leo   They use earth movers.

Martin   I could dig.

Leo   Nowadays road building's all about planning.

Paulina   You'll want beer.

Leo   Ask yourself what the road's for.

Paulina   When you do father and son things you always want beer.

Leo   A beer would be nice.

Paulina   There isn't any.

Leo   You ask yourself. Who's going to use this road? Why? What do they need? How can it be more beautiful? That's what the job's about, that's what men like me, and you, are for, Martin . . . we ask questions . . . you understand?

They dig for some moments in silence.

Martin   Actually, I'm bored of this.

Martin *stops.*

Leo   You've only just started.

Martin   Sorry.

Leo (*to* **Paulina**)   I thought you were getting beers.

Martin   For a minute I thought I would . . .
But then I seemed to get bored.

Leo   He wants a beer.

Martin   Digging wasn't that interesting after all.

Leo   That's what I'm telling you. It's the planning that's interesting, the questions . . .

Martin   Sorry, Boss.
Maybe I'm just not cut out for work.
I have to go.

Paulina   You're not coming into the house.

Martin   I'll be late.

Leo   Martin.

Martin   See you later.

Martin *exits through the house.*

Leo   You could have given him a drink.

Paulina   He didn't want a drink.

Leo   Of course he did. It's a warm day. He wanted a cold beer. I want a cold beer.

Paulina   You wanted a beer. He wanted to dig.
. . .
Do you know they use fish brains in beer?

Leo   Fish heads.

Paulina   No wonder it makes people violent.
Men urinating in the street.
Women stumbling around like retarded people.
Considering what they put in it, it's no wonder.

They hear the sound of the doorbell. Neither of them move. After a moment **Dorothy** *enters.*

Dorothy   There's a woman here to see you.

Leo   Who?

Paulina   A woman?

Dorothy   Mackie she said.

Leo   Christ.

Dorothy   Will I tell her you're busy?

Leo   No. No. Bring her through.

Dorothy *exits.*

Leo   Business.

Paulina   Shame.

Sheena *enters with* **Dorothy**.

Sheena   This is lovely. What a lovely house you've got, Mr Black. Did you build it?

Leo   No.

Sheena   And this is your . . . backyard?

Dorothy   It's a patio actually.

Sheena   For sitting out?

Paulina   It's easier to clean.

Sheena   Of course it is. I'd love a patio. You don't get much chance to sit out where I am. You must be Mrs Black.

Paulina   Paulina.

Sheena   Sheena Mackie.

Leo   You always seem to find me at weekends, Ms Mackie.

Sheena   I've got a job. I have to work in the week. And this is your daughter?

Dorothy   Dorothy.

Sheena   The girl I talked to on the phone?

Leo   Dorothy is also my secretary.

Sheena   A family business. That's nice. We hardly need introduced, do we? We've chatted so often.

Leo   Why don't you get us some tea, Dorothy? If you'll allow me to get changed, Ms Mackie, I'll be with you in a moment.

Leo *and* **Dorothy** *exit.* **Paulina** *continues potting plants.* **Sheena** *stands silent.*

Paulina   I've always thought it would be nice to live in a tall building.

Sheena   Oh?

Paulina   Is it nice?

Sheena   Nice? Not really. Not nice. No.

Paulina   Are you scared of heights?

Sheena   Height's not really the problem.

Paulina   Oh no. Height's a strong point. You don't want to be in amongst it.

Sheena   Amongst it?

Paulina   Ground floors attract opportunist thieves. I don't imagine they bother with the tenth. On the tenth you can watch it all happening down below. Rise above it all. Do you watch?

Sheena   Sometimes. Sometimes I can't avoid it. Sometimes I'm in amongst it myself.

3

Billy *and* **Martin** *on top of a tall building. Daytime.* **Billy** *pointing.*

Billy   There . . . to the left.

Martin   Where?

Billy   Follow my finger.

Martin   There's only tower blocks.

Billy   That's it . . . there see.

Martin   There?

Billy   Third along.

Martin   You live there?

Billy   Yeah.

Martin   Christ.

Billy   What d'you mean, Christ?

Martin   I mean . . . Christ. Isn't it supposed to be . . . I've never been. I thought you were showing because . . .

Billy   I'm showing you because it's where I live.

Martin   I've never. I haven't seen any of those places . . . close up. I mean.

Billy   Where do you live?

Martin   You can't see it from here.

Billy   Is it a flat?

Martin   No.

Billy   A house.

Martin   Yes.

Billy   Is it detached or part of a street?

Martin   Detached. Do we have to talk about this?

Billy   Nice area?

Martin   If you like nice areas.

Billy   Can I visit?

Martin   When I was a student I lived in a squat.

Billy   Can I visit?

Martin   No.

Billy *starts to walk along the edge of the roof. Calmly balancing.*

Billy   Why not? You can visit me.

Martin   So. Don't do that.

Billy   Visit me. On my dangerous estate.

Martin   You'll fall off.

Billy   It's like Beirut you know. War zone.

Martin   Is it?

Billy   Is it fuck.

Martin   I said don't do that.

Billy   You're scared.

Martin   Probably better than where I stay anyway.

Billy   How's that?

Martin   I don't know. It probably is.

Billy   How's it better?

Martin   The people probably. Probably the atmosphere. Isn't it supposed to be better. Neighbours talk to each other. I don't know. How should I know?

. . .

Will you fucking stop doing that? It makes me nervous.

Billy *stops walking along the roof edge.*

Billy   Can I visit yours then?

Martin   I won't be there long anyway.

Billy   You moving?

Martin   Leaving.

Billy   Leaving what?

Martin   Home. I can't stick it.
The city. The country. All of it.
I'm off.

Billy   Where to?

Martin   Canada. I don't know. Albania maybe. Maybe
Fife. Some wilderness. Somewhere with mountains.

Billy   A holiday?

Martin   Escape.

Billy   What have you got to escape from?

Martin   You wouldn't understand.

Billy   Maybe I would.

Martin   I need a change.

Billy   I like you as you are.

Martin   You're shit, you'll take anything.

Billy   I take what I want.

Martin   I'm fucking off. On my own. No people. No talk.
No things.

Billy   I'll come with you.

Martin   No, you won't.

Billy   Why not?

Martin   I don't want you to come.

Billy   Yes, you do.

Martin   You'd only talk. When people talk they clog your
head with shit. The shit they talk gets in your head and slops
around. More and more shit. Television schedules. Opinions
about sport. Property prices. It all slops around until
eventually it slops out your mouth and back into someone
else's head.

Billy   You're fucked up?

Martin   Course I'm fucked up.

Billy   We've got something in common then.
I'm fucked up as well.

Martin   No, you're not.

Billy   I try to run off the top of buildings.

Martin   That's natural. You're poor.
. . .
I just can't . . . I'm not . . . not any more.
. . .
I need to get pure. I got off on the wrong foot somewhere.
Somewhere around when I was born. Now I need to go back.
Go back get clean and start again.
. . .
I'm going to learn to make furniture.

Billy   I'd like to do that.

Martin   If I go to the country somewhere. I could find
some old guy in the mountains that does it.

Billy   Yeah!

Martin   An old guy with a fat old wife.

Billy   Yeah!

Martin   He might be deaf. A deaf couple.

Billy   An apprentice.

Martin   He'll show me what to do with signs. I'll learn how
to turn wood and make tables.

Billy   The two of us.

Martin   I'm going alone.
I've got it all planned. I'm just going to set off and walk.
Just head in that direction and not stop.

He points.

Billy   That's the sea.

Martin   That way then.

Billy   Bathgate. No mountains there.

Martin   Fuck off.

Billy   I'll follow you.

Martin   I'll run.

Billy   I'll chase you.

Martin   I'll kill you.

Billy   Have you told your mum and dad?

Martin   I'll leave a note.

Billy   They'll worry.

Martin   It's for the best.

Billy   They'll be hurt.

Martin   Don't try and tell me what they'll feel. You haven't a fucking clue.

Billy   Neither have you.

Martin   I know exactly what they'll feel. I know precisely. I can feel it for them. Better than them.
They'll feel pain.
A great amount of pain.

Billy   So stay.

Martin   I don't like them.

Billy   So. Stick it.

Martin   The longer I stay the more I want to hurt them.

Billy   Everyone gets that. That's not special.

Martin   Stay or go. Makes no difference. Either way there'll be a great amount of pain.

Billy   Martin.
I don't want you to go without me.

Martin   You can't come.

Billy   I'll miss you.

Martin   So.

Billy   I'll feel a great amount of pain.

Martin   You attached yourself to me. If you attach yourself to someone like me you deserve pain. I have to go away and make furniture for a while. If I make furniture in a lonely place for long enough then maybe, I'll become a good person.

Billy   You believe that?

Martin   Of course I fucking don't.

Billy   Why say it then?

Martin   It's the only thing I can think of.

Billy *takes* **Martin**'s *head in his hands, suddenly. Turns his face towards him.*

Martin   Fuck off.

Billy   Look at me.

Martin   Stop it.

Billy   Look at me.

Martin *is struggling but* **Billy** *is stronger. He holds on.* **Martin** *gives up struggling.*

Billy   I can make you good.
Me.
You cunt.
Me.
Billy.
Understand?
I can make you good.

Billy *lets go.*

4

Sheena, Paulina, Leo *and* **Dorothy** *inside the house. A model of Eden Court is on the table by* **Leo**. **Sheena** *is examining the model.*

Sheena   This one's mine.

Leo   I realise the current fashion's against high-rise building, Mrs Mackie.

Sheena   Sheena.

Leo   Of course, Sheena. Dorothy. Will you offer Sheena some tea?

Dorothy *doesn't move.*

Sheena   Wait a minute. Is it this one? One balcony's much the same as any other, isn't it? Have you put all the windows in?

Leo   Paulina, you don't need to stay. If you don't want to. This is work.

Paulina   I'm interested.

Sheena   It could be any one of these. It depends on which way round you stand.

Paulina   I'm interested in your buildings.

Leo   Fine. Whatever.

Sheena   Something's different. The shape of it . . . colour or something . . .

Leo   It's an exact model, Mrs Mackie, an exact model of the Eden Court design. I wanted you to see this to make a point.

Sheena   The grass. You've made the grass green. Put green felt down.

Dorothy   That's the convention. All models do that.

Leo   This is the original design. Six standing towers. Aerial walkways linking each tower, platforms linking each balcony. The whole enclosing a central park . . .

Sheena   It shouldn't be green. That part of the estate's all mud now. It catches the rain. It's like a draining bowl. You want to put down brown felt for that.

Dorothy   The models aren't supposed to be realistic. They're impressions . . .

Leo   The original design was, in fact, loosely based on Stonehenge.

Paulina   I didn't think anyone lived in Stonehenge.

Leo   Standing stones were the inspiration.

Paulina   Too draughty I thought.

Sheena   Didn't you win an award for this?

Dorothy   He did.

Leo   I won some recognition at the time.

Sheena   It looks good. From this angle. From above.

Dorothy   It's about space. Architecture's about shaping space. If you look at it from here you can see how he's moulding a communal space . . .

Sheena   Were the judges in a helicopter when they gave you the award?

Leo   I was asked to build cheap homes. Cheap housing. High density accommodation . . . Eden Court is a council estate, Mrs Mackie, but I built connecting areas, and public spaces, I designed it so everyone's front room gets the sun at certain times of the day . . . They're not luxury homes, but architecturally, they're well designed. That's the point I'm making. I put as much imagination, as much thought, as much of myself into these buildings as any . . .

Dorothy   I think they're beautiful.

Leo   Objectively, aesthetically, functionally . . . Eden Court is a good estate.

Sheena   People are queueing up to leave.

Dorothy   It's a free country.

Sheena   They're unhappy. They get depressed. They get ill.
The place they live in makes them depressed.
Do you understand that?
Do you understand how important that is?

Leo   It's mass housing. You can't build mass housing to suit individual desires. It doesn't matter who designs it. You can knock it down if you want to but the problems will still be there. There'll still be unemployment, there'll still be poverty. If you want to change your circumstances Mrs Mackie.

Sheena   Sheena.

Leo   I suggest you vote labour.
I do.

Sheena   Would you say Eden Court was yours? Your building?

Leo   I designed it.

Sheena   Would you say it was your responsibility?

Leo   It was my responsibility. It's not my fault the council turned it into a ghetto. I didn't put the people in it.

Sheena   Were you there when the flats were built?

Leo   I supervised the project.

Sheena   Did you actually supervise the work? Watch every bolt go in? See every panel in place . . . ?

Leo   Of course not.

Sheena   Build them high, build them quick and build them cheap. That was the idea, wasn't it?

Leo   Not my idea.

Sheena   No, but it was the commission, wasn't it . . . what you were told?

Leo   They were designed to be built easily.

Sheena   Built in factories. Pre-cast.

Leo   It's a simple method.

Sheena   Easy to skimp on as well. Difficult to check up on mistakes.

Leo   I didn't hire the contractors.

Sheena   A few bolts missing here and there. They always over-design these things anyway. If the odd panel doesn't fit, never mind.

Leo   I admit there was a lack of supervision but the contractors were under pressure. Time was a pressure. You may not remember but it was you people who were demanding the houses.

Paulina   That's not how I remember it.

Leo   What?

Paulina   I remember you talking about it. At the time. You said the job was rushed. You said it was a scandal . . .

Leo   I'm not sure you know what you're talking about, Paulina.

Paulina   She does.

Sheena   I don't mean to seem rude, Mr Black. You're probably a nice man. You've a nice family. You probably meant for it to be a nice place to live. Isn't that what architects are for? I remember the brochures we got. A drawing of the sun shining and kids playing in the park. When they came round looking for tenants I signed like that. I saw the models. But it was all 'vision', wasn't it? Vision's the word you would use. Not houses, but a vision of housing. Everyone nicely boxed away. Cheaply accommodated. Eden Court might look like Stonehenge to you, it might have won an award but it's build like a pack of cards.

Leo   It's secure. It won't fall down.

Sheena   Boxes piled one on top of the other and we're stuffed in them like exhibits. You weren't asked to design houses, you were asked to house people, there's a world of difference.

Dorothy   That's rubbish. It's rubbish. I've already told her she's talking rubbish, Dad.

Leo   Dorothy, I think you've said enough.

Sheena   The local authority can't afford to admit the mistakes. The contractors have money. They'd probably be happy to go to court. The whole thing could take years. We don't have years. We're just ordinary people who would like decent places to live. If you give us your support they can't ignore us.

Leo   I won't lie about my own building.

Sheena   It's not your building though, is it? It never was. You just did the frippery bits that win prizes. Your stuff's just the façade. Take it away and the place is a dormitory block. Stonehenge, communal space, it doesn't mean anything if there isn't life in the place – shops, work, kids, pubs . . .

Leo   There was supposed to be . . .

Sheena   But there wasn't.

Leo   So destroy it. Blame the building. Wipe it out.

Sheena   Architecture's for the people who pay. Always. All we want to do is take control. It's not about good or bad buildings, it's about who decides. Don't we have the right to not like good buildings? You do.

Leo   I think we're agreed this is not my problem.

Sheena   But you can solve it.

Leo   I don't see why I should.

Sheena   Because it would be a good thing.

Leo   I can't help you. I'm sorry. I won't see good ideas blown up just because some people can't see beyond their own misery.

Paulina   I think you should knock them down.

Dorothy   Mum.

Paulina   If that's what people want.
At least they know what they want.
If they're sure. Then it's cruel, isn't it?

To stop them just because of history, or how things were
supposed to be. The intention.
I think you should help them.

Leo   This is about work, Paulina. This is about destroying
my work.

Sheena   I'm sorry you couldn't help us.
If you change your mind you know where to find me.

Paulina   Don't go. Why don't you stay ... for lunch ...
I was making lunch.

Sheen   Thank you but ... I think I should go.
I can find my own way out.

Sheena *leaves.*

Leo   You're supposed to support me.

Paulina   I thought she was right. I thought she won the
argument.

Leo   That isn't the point. You're my wife.

Paulina *leaves.*

Leo   Well, you can forget your fucking patio.
Paulina.
You can forget your fucking patio.
Do you hear me?

Dorothy   Don't worry about it, Dad. She's mad.
Nobody's going to knock it down.
Anyone can see she's mad.

Leo   Why didn't you give me her letters?

Dorothy   They were rubbish. I told you ...

Leo   Why didn't you give me them?

Dorothy   I told you ... They were just ... I didn't want
you to worry.

Leo   What's wrong with you, Dorothy?

Dorothy   Dad.

Leo   Did you think I'd made a mistake?

Dorothy   I thought . . .

Leo   I'm your father, Dorothy. I'm your employer.
How dare you humiliate me like that.
Did you think I'd built it badly?

Dorothy   No.

Leo   Did you think that was possible.

Dorothy   Please.

Leo   There was no mistake.

Dorothy   I know.

Leo   The structure is sound.

Dorothy   I know.

Leo   No mistake.

Leo *picks up the model and leaves the room. A wave of nausea passes over* **Dorothy**. **Paulina** *enters.*

Paulina   Are you sick?

Dorothy   No.

Paulina   You look like you're going to be sick.

Dorothy   I'm all right.

Paulina   Shall I bring water?

Dorothy   I'm not going to be sick.

Paulina   You're not pregnant, are you?

Dorothy   What?

Paulina   If you've got nausea.

Dorothy   I'm not pregnant.

Paulina   How do you know?

Dorothy   I know.

Paulina   Did you test yourself?

Dorothy   I know.

Paulina   Maybe you should test yourself.
You look pale.
Your complexion's . . .
There's a spot. It might be hormonal.

Dorothy   Why did you do that, Mum?

Paulina   Do what?

Dorothy   Behave like that. In front of that woman. Why?

Paulina   How did I behave?

Dorothy   As though you were neurotic. You behaved as
though you were neurotic.

Paulina   I only said . . .

Dorothy   He was humiliated. In front of . . .

Paulina   I only said . . .

Dorothy   In front of everyone . . .

Paulina   I was commenting on . . .

Dorothy   You made him look small.

Paulina   What she said. The woman.

Dorothy   In front of . . .

Paulina   It made sense.

Dorothy   In front of me.
You didn't need to . . .
There was no need.

Paulina   I'm sorry. I didn't mean . . .

Dorothy   Tell him that. Say sorry to him.

Paulina *approaches* **Dorothy**. *Tries to touch her.*

Paulina   Dorothy.

Dorothy   Why do you have to make him . . .
Why can't you be decent to him?
You used to be decent to him.

Paulina   It's difficult . . .

Dorothy   Try.

Paulina   It's complicated. You wouldn't . . .

Dorothy   Explain.

Paulina   I really think it's best left between . . .

Dorothy   Tell me.

Paulina   I don't see what's to be gained from digging around in . . .

Dorothy   Tell me.

Paulina   In exploring this . . . landscape. Really, it's not interesting. I promise you. This situation between your father and me. It's quite . . .

Dorothy   What?

Paulina   Mundane.

Dorothy   What?

Paulina   I have no . . .
So embarrassing really.
No admiration for him.

Pause. **Dorothy** *turns away from her. Silent. Holding back tears.*

Paulina   No feeling . . .

Dorothy   Not good enough.

Paulina   It stopped. It just finished.

Dorothy   Not good enough.

Paulina   I look at him now. I can't bear to . . .

Dorothy   Selfish.

Paulina   The way he . . .

Dorothy   Selfish.

Paulina   He looks so . . . failed.

Dorothy   Selfish cow. You're a . . .

Paulina   It's not like that.

Dorothy   Selfish bloody cow.
Selfish self-centred bloody cow.
. . .
Sorry.

Paulina   It can change, Dorothy. It can just . . .

Dorothy   He's the same. He's the same man.
He needs you.

Paulina   I know.
But it can't be like that any more.
I'm sorry.
. . .
You look pale.

Dorothy   I'm fine.

Paulina   You need to look after yourself.

Dorothy   I'm all right.

Paulina   If you worry, if you upset yourself, it shows in
your skin, you know. It shows itself.

Dorothy   Mum, please, just leave me alone.

Paulina   You used to have such a clear complexion. Hot
water. A glass of hot water. Every evening. It's cleansing. It
has a cleansing effect.

Dorothy   Go away, Mum. Please.

Paulina   You know it's not my fault. Don't you, Dorothy?

Dorothy   What does that mean?

Paulina   Nothing. It means it's not my fault.

5

Darkness. The sound of a motorway. Traffic passing. **Dorothy** *is
hitching. Lights pass her but no one stops.*

6

Martin *and* **Billy** *on a muddy patch of grass in Eden Court.*
Martin *is wearing the green jacket.*

Billy   This is it. This is where I'm from.

Martin   Nice.

Billy   Don't look so nervous.

Martin   I'm not nervous.

Billy   Your hands are shaking.

Billy *touches his hand.*

Martin   Piss off.

A sudden bang. It echoes. **Martin** *throws himself to the ground.*

Billy   Air-gun.

Martin   I wasn't. I just wanted to sit down.

Billy   You'll spoil your jacket. You don't know what you'll
pick up.

Martin   Seems all right to me.

Billy   Eight blocks. They're all the same. In a big circle.
You're supposed to be able to tell the time from the shadows.

Martin   Can you?

Billy   I don't know. I can only tell the time digital.
Apparently the architect committed suicide when he saw
how it turned out. It's supposed to be built backwards or
something. Probably found out it told the time backwards
and topped himself.
So what do you think?

Martin   Can't you leave?

Billy   Not unless I'm thrown out. If I got thrown out I
could be rehoused.

Martin   You could get a job.

Billy   So could you.

Martin   I don't want one.

Billy   Neither do I.

Martin   I thought you wanted to work. I thought that was the problem. I thought you people wanted jobs.

Billy   We have to say that.

Martin   I thought . . .

Billy   Why should I want a job? You don't. I couldn't put up with this place and a job as well. I'd die.

Martin   So what d'you do all day?

Billy   I'm like one of those flies. You know those flies that are born and breed and die all in one day but to the fly that day's a lifetime? That's me. Skating across the water for an afternoon.

Martin   I don't know how you can stand it.

Billy   I didn't say I could.

Martin   I don't know how anyone could.

Billy   Maybe we're a new species. Like the cockroaches.

Martin   Why did you bring me here?

Billy   It's where I'm from. I wanted you to see.

Martin   Are you trying to make some point?

Billy   No.

Martin   Make me feel something.

Billy   Martin, we could go somewhere. Both of us. We could both just . . . fuck off.
If we went away together.

Martin   We won't.

Billy   But if we did. We could even go abroad. You've got money. I could work. In a foreign country I could work. We could just get on a train now. Get on a train and fuck off to the sunshine. You and me.

Martin   No.

Billy   Think about it. Greece. Spain. Italy. Amsterdam. You and me. People think about it but nobody does it. We could make furniture together.

Martin   Making furniture was my idea.

Billy   I could have my own idea.

Martin   You took me here to say this, didn't you?

Billy   Think about it. We could learn the language. Eat the food. Work. Sun. Dress in Italian clothes. We could do it.

Martin   You had it all planned.

Billy   Think about it.

Martin   Make me feel bad. Make me save you.

Billy   It's not like that. It's an idea.

Martin   What do you think I am?
The White Knight of the Lavatories?
Sir Galahad of The Gents?

Billy   You need me.

Martin   In your dreams.

Billy   I like you, Martin.

Martin   So?

Billy   *Nobody else does.*

7

Dorothy *is sitting in her bedroom, in front of the mirror, in her underwear.* **Leo** *enters without knocking.* **Dorothy** *instinctively covers up.*

Leo   Oh. I'm sorry. Can I come in?

Dorothy   Dad.

Leo   I just thought I'd . . .

Dorothy   Do you want the seat?

Leo   I'll crouch. That's what I'll do. I'll crouch beside you. Dorothy, I . . .

He reaches out to touch her and then withdraws his hand.

I'm sorry about earlier on.

Dorothy   It's fine.

Leo   I shouldn't have shouted. I was.

Dorothy   Honestly, it's fine.

Leo   You know I love you.

Dorothy   Do you want a drink?

Leo   Sorry?

Dorothy   A lemonade? I want a lemonade. I made some. Do you want me to get you one?

Dorothy *is about to get up and go.*

Leo   Wait.
It's all right.

Dorothy   I'll get that drink, shall I?

Leo   I need to know something.
You and I . . .
We do . . . like each other, don't we?

Dorothy   I'm parched actually. (*She coughs.*)

Leo   We're friends.

Dorothy   Friends. Yes.

Leo   You're sure?

Dorothy   Course I'm sure. I think I will have that lemonade after all.

Leo   Don't go yet.

Dorothy   Whatever.

Leo   You see, Dorothy.
This is difficult for me to say.
But . . .

I feel slightly . . . alone.
At the moment.

Dorothy   Oh.

Leo   I'm telling you this because . . .
Well, because things are . . .
Martin . . . your mother. I can't seem to talk to them . . .

Dorothy   I told you. You're my dad.

Leo   I want you to know that I love you.

Dorothy   Dad, I'm sorry. I don't want to seem. It's your business, isn't it? You and Mum. I'm glad you feel you can talk to me. I love you. You love me. It's difficult to talk about that sort of thing so the effort is . . . appreciated. But you don't have to say it. That's the nice thing about families, isn't it? You just know. You don't always have to say.

Leo   Martin isn't going to work for me, is he?
He's going to go away.

Dorothy   You don't know. He might . . .

Leo   As a father sometimes.
You think you might have made the wrong choices.
You want to ask.

Dorothy   He said he was interested.

Leo   No.

Dorothy   Time. He needs . . .

Leo   You think if you could go back . . .
I've been thinking . . .
If I could go back.
Go back to the point where the mistake happened.

Dorothy   Oh God.

Leo   What?

Dorothy   I can't.

Leo   Can't what?

Dorothy   This conversation.
Can't do it. Sorry.

Leo   I feel lost, Dorothy.
I've no plans for this.
It's not part of the design.
Tell me the truth, Dorothy . . .
Does he hate me?
Does he despise me?

Dorothy   As a matter of fact I feel very thirsty now.

She puts on her dressing-gown and leaves.

8

The sudden, loud blast of a lorry's horn. **Joe** *is in his cab driving. The radio is turned up loud. It is playing 'From Boulder to Birmingham' sung by Emmylou Harris.* **Joe** *is playing with the steering wheel.*

Joe   Pooooow Pooooow Poooooow.

9

Martin *and* **Billy** *in a gay bar. In the background a pub quiz is going on.*

Martin   Stop sulking. You took me here. I got you a drink. Fucking drink it.

Paulina *and* **Leo** *have just had sex.* **Leo** *is still in the bed.* **Paulina** *is sitting nearby.*

Leo   Do you mind if I have a cigarette?
. . .
It's been a long time.
. . .

Voice   Number Fifteen.
Pencils at the ready. Boys and Girls.
Who played the male and female leads in a. *Pretty Woman*, b. *Pretty in Pink* and c. *Pink Flamingos*?

Billy Richard Gere, Julia Roberts . . .

Martin You know that?

Billy Put the answers down.

Leo *lights up a cigarette.*

Leo I'm glad it happened. It needed to happen. I'm glad you . . .

Paulina It was interesting.

Leo More than interesting.

Martin *and* **Billy**.

Martin I can't believe you know that.

Billy Hand it in.

Paulina *and* **Leo**.

Paulina It was an experiment. The results were interesting.

Leo An experiment? You're my wife.

Paulina I wish you wouldn't call me that.

Leo Christ, not this again.

Paulina Wife, it's so bovine. Husband. It's all so agricultural.

Billy *and* **Martin**.

Voice Staying with pretty women . . . who had a hit with 'Oh Pretty Woman' . . . there are options in this question.

Billy Roy Orbison.

Voice You may prefer to wait for your options.

Billy It's Roy Orbison.

Martin He said you may prefer . . .

Billy Just put it down.

Voice Just to remind you, boys and girls, the prizes tonight are champagne, a bottle of crème de menthe and a five-pound voucher for I.G. Mellis.

Billy *has written the answer.*

Billy   Give it in.

Leo *and* **Paulina**.

Leo   Paulina.

Paulina   Have you noticed? When you can't think of anything else to say you say 'Paulina'.

Leo   Why are you spoiling this?

Paulina   You want me to be touched. Moved. As though your voice making that sound might stir me up.

Leo   Doesn't it?

Paulina   No. That's the interesting thing. Paulina. It feels like it isn't my name any more. Feels more connected with you now than with me.

Leo   What then?
What can I say to stir you up?

Paulina   Dressing-table. Bedroom. Husband. Living-room. Sofa. Carpet. Wall.

Leo   What?

Paulina   Window. Floor. Laundry basket.

Leo   Paulina.

Paulina   Dinner party. Garden. Cheeseboard. Paulina.

Leo   Are you having a breakdown? Is that what this is?

Paulina   Making love. Making love.

Leo   I thought you wanted . . . You asked me.

Paulina   You find yourself amongst these words.
You find these words being used.
You begin to notice. People say them without blinking.

Leo   You've lost me. You have to explain this.

Paulina   Everyone wants me to explain.

Leo   We go to bed in the middle of the afternoon. It's wonderful. We make up. Everything's better and then you start having some kind of breakdown. You could at least try to explain . . .

Paulina *and* **Leo**.

Paulina   I have to ask you to leave Leo.

Leo   . . .

Paulina   The house. I mean.

Leo   What the hell am I supposed to have done?

Paulina   I realise it's your house as much as it's mine. More maybe. But I'd like you to leave it. Would you do that for me? As a gesture of affection. You're not an unusually cruel man. You'd be better at living somewhere else than me.

Leo   For Christ's sake. It's not gone that far, has it?

Paulina   It will.

Leo   A trial separation.

Paulina   Not trial. A separation.

Leo   You want to throw away a marriage. Just like that.

Paulina   Not 'throw away'. Those are the wrong words.

Leo   I'm sorry. I don't have a thesaurus.

Paulina   If you could throw it away, forget it, start again etc. All those things but . . . go back to a time before it happened and follow a different route but . . . wherever I go now, for the rest of my life I'll take this marriage with me. For better or worse. I'm not throwing it away.

Leo   Why now? More than twenty years you've had, and now, today you say it's a mistake . . . why not yesterday, why not years ago?

Paulina   Fear.

Leo   Fear? Afraid of me? Don't make me laugh.

Paulina   Afraid of me. Afraid there wasn't any of me left. Afraid I'd eroded.

. . .

I am trying, Leo . . .

Does that explain it?

Leo   No, it fucking doesn't.

Paulina   Don't you feel it? Feel yourself eroding?

Leo   No. No, I don't.

Paulina   Really?

Leo   Really.

Paulina   That's interesting.

Billy *and* **Martin**.

Billy   Wait a minute wait . . .

Ahhh . . . It's coming . . .

Rick Alessi.

Rick Alessi, Sharon Watts and Sinbad.

Martin *writes the answers down.*

Martin   How can you fill your head with this shit?

I can't believe this amount of shit can be in one head.

Billy   Just put the answer in.

Martin   Why don't we go somewhere else?

Billy   I'm winning.

Voice   Born in 1908, Indiana, Pennsylvania. No longer alive or active in the field in which he or she first found fame.

Billy   Fuck.

Martin   I'm leaving.

Billy   Film star. Film star . . . think . . .

Martin   I said, let's go.

Leo *and* **Paulina**.

Leo   I'm sorry.

Paulina Don't apologise.

Leo I'm sorry.

Paulina You haven't done anything wrong.

Leo I didn't see.

Paulina You're just part of a situation.

Billy *and* **Martin**.

Billy Bette Davis!

Martin You coming then.

Billy Wait though, too early for Bette Davis.

Leo *and* **Paulina**.

Paulina You're part of a situation that developed. That's all. Not your fault.

Leo I mean more to you than that.
I think you forget sometimes, Paulina, that I know you. I know you better than anyone.

Paulina You know your wife. When you leave you'll notice a wife-shaped space.

Billy *and* **Martin**.

Voice You may want to wait for your options.

Billy Leave if you want to.

Martin You haven't finished your drink.

Leo *and* **Paulina**.

Leo We need to have fun again. That's all it is. We stopped having fun. Kids and everything. Responsibility. Changes you. We need to rekindle . . . get back, and . . . I can't believe you feel nothing. I can't believe there's nothing there.

Paulina There's knowledge. I know you. Knowledge and a sort of disgust. The sort of disgust a prisoner feels for a cell mate. That's all.

Billy *and* **Martin**.

Billy   Jimmy Stewart!

Martin   What?

Billy   *It's a Wonderful Life!*

Martin   Hardly.

Billy   Take it up to him. Go on.

Leo *and* **Paulina**.

Leo   Does it matter that I still love you?

Paulina   Sadly. No.

Leo   That I need you.

Paulina   Sorry.

Billy *and* **Martin**.

Billy   I won the crème de menthe.
Have it.
It goes with your jacket.

Martin   Can we go now?

Billy   If you want.

10

Darkness. The sound of traffic passing on a motorway. **Dorothy**
hitching. No lorry stops. She clutches herself.

11

Sunset. **Leo**, *holding his car keys, is standing on the balcony of an Eden
Court block.* **Sheena** *next to him.*

Sheena   You can see your new site, from here.
I've watched it. Watched the cranes pull it all up.
Watched the wrecking ball.
It looks pretty from a distance. The docks and everything.
The water in the background. It's pretty.

It looks nice with the sunset.
When I first lived here I watched the ships.
Watched the men loading and unloading.
Cars and crates of whisky, loads of coal and sacks of bananas.
I thought it was a privilege. Living above the docks.
Watching over the city's front door. And then the front door closed.
Containers.
You know the containers you put on ships, on lorries . . .
As soon as they invented containers there was no need for docks in the city centre. No need for dockers. A port and a motorway's all you need. The crane lifts the box out of the ship and onto the back of the truck. Done.
So the dockers and the sailors lost their jobs and you got yours . . . making museums and restaurants out of warehouses and whisky bonds.
Even the tarts moved inland.
All that got left here was people who were stuck.
Stuck in boxes on the dockside waiting to be picked up.
Hoping someone's going to stop for us and take us with them.

12

The roof of a tall building. Sunset. **Billy** *and* **Martin**. **Billy** *is drinking crème de menthe.*

Billy   Just exactly what is it that you want to do?
We wanna be free.
We wanna do what we wanna do.
And we wanna get loaded.
And we wanna have a good time.

Billy *mimes air guitar.* **Billy** *moves to touch* **Martin**. **Martin** *turns him away.*

Martin   Stand still.

Billy   I want to touch you.

Martin   You can't.

Billy   I want to.

Martin   Stop talking.

A pause. **Martin** *unbuckles* **Billy**'*s belt and pulls his jeans down. Still standing behind him, he looks at* **Billy***.*

Martin   Pull your shirt over your head.

Billy *does this. He is about to take the T-shirt completely off when* **Martin** *stops him.*

Martin   Leave it there. Keep your hands there. Keep your face covered.

Billy *stands still.* **Martin** *finally moves towards* **Billy** *and embraces him. Still from behind. Wanking him off.*

13

Leo *and* **Sheena** *on the balcony of Eden Court.*

Leo   Have you a family, Sheena?

Sheena   I have a son.

Leo   Grown up?

Sheena   He's dead. Same age as yours. Elliot. He was named after Elliot Gould. Does that make you laugh?

Leo   No.

Sheena   It makes me laugh. Makes me cringe to think about it.

Leo   How did he die?

Sheena   He stepped off the balcony.
I was in the kitchen. He was watching telly.
I came through and he wasn't there.
I thought he'd gone out.
They didn't know who he was when they found him.
They had to knock on all the doors in the block to see who was missing.

He was depressed. If you're depressed and there's a high balcony, apparently it's a red rag to a bull.

Leo   I'm sorry.

Sheena   Not your fault. He was depressed.

Leo   This place'd be enough to depress anybody.

Sheena   He was depressed. Elliot wasn't special. People jump here all the time. That's the trouble with architects. You think you're responsible for everything. You think it's all under your doing. You don't think this campaign's about Elliot, do you?

Leo   I don't know. Is it?

Sheena   You're not God, Mr Black. You're an architect. God's a different campaign altogether. This is about housing . . . it's about people having an effect . . .

Leo   A destructive effect.

Sheena   Maybe.

Leo   They've blown up others. They blew up one in Glasgow and they're blowing them up in Hackney. I don't suppose anyone'll miss this place. I don't even know if I will.

Sheena   Why did you come here, Mr Black?

Leo   To talk to you.

Sheena   What did you want to say?

Leo   I just wanted to explain . . . the idea . . . the dream behind this mess. It was a good . . . It wasn't malicious.

Sheena   You wanted me to tell you you were a nice man.

Leo   No . . .
Yes.

Sheena   It doesn't matter. Whether you're a nice man or not doesn't matter.

Leo   It does to me.

Sheena   I can't help you with that.

Leo   The new place, if they build it, it'll be exactly the same, you know.

Sheena   I'm not stupid. I'm not a silly wee woman who doesn't like modern buildings. You're right. I know this is 'good design'. 'Good design' isn't the point. The point is control. Who has the power to knock down and who has the power to build.

Leo   Even if it's wrong.

Sheena   Even if it's wrong.

14

Billy, *alone, walking along the edge of the roof, drinking crème de menthe.*

Darkness.

15

Leo, Paulina *and* **Dorothy** *having a meal. Silence.* **Martin** *enters.*

Martin   Any for me, Boss? I'm famished.

Leo   Sit down, Martin.

Martin   Oh. It's one of those.

Dorothy   Just sit down, will you?

Martin   The old family talk.

Leo   There's something you ought to know.

Martin   Fire away.

Leo   Your mother and I . . .

Paulina   Your father's leaving.

Martin   Oh.

Leo   Temporarily. We've decided. There's been, a tension, I'm sure you've noticed.

Martin   What do you want me to say?

Leo   This doesn't affect you, of course, this is still your home . . .

Martin   Am I supposed to say something?

Paulina   Say what you want to say.

Dorothy   Does anybody want any water?

Leo   If you want to talk about it. Of course we can talk about it.
Do you? Do you want to talk about it?

Martin   . . .
No.

Dorothy   Anyone? Water?

Leo   We'll still be a family, of course. Obviously we still . . . both of us . . . still love . . .

Martin   What about money?

Dorothy   Martin.

Martin   I'm sorry. I didn't mean to say that. I meant . . .

Leo   I don't think you need to worry about money.

Martin   Sorry.

Silence.

What are you going to do?

Paulina   What do you mean?

Martin   Now. What are you going to do. Take up singing? Hang-glide? Take a lover? Fulfil those buried dreams?

Paulina   Don't be crass.

Martin   What then?

Dorothy   If you don't mind I'll . . .

Paulina   Nothing in particular.

Dorothy   I'd like to go now. If you want me to stay I can stay . . .

Martin   Nothing in particular. All this for nothing in particular.

Dorothy   If there's anything I can do.
Is there?

Martin   Seems a bit drastic.

Dorothy   There's nothing I can do. So if you don't mind I'll go out for a while.

Paulina   You don't have to go.

Dorothy   I do.

Martin   Me too, in fact . . . said I'd be somewhere . . .

Leo   We need to talk about the future.

Martin   Who gets what?

Leo   The future, Martin . . .

Martin   Oh. I'd rather . . .
I don't know the way to speak in these situations.
Do you?
I'll only say the wrong thing again. Have the wrong idea.
I'd rather leave you to it.

Dorothy and **Martin** *leave*.

Leo   Martin!

Paulina   Leave them.

Leo   We can't just . . .

Paulina   Leave them.

16

The roof. **Martin** *wearing the green jacket carrying a small rucksack. An empty bottle of crème de menthe. The sound of an ambulance below.*

Martin   Billy?
Billy?
Where are you?
Billy . . .
Let's go . . .
We're going to Fife, Billy.
Billy?
Fuck.

Darkness.

17

Leo *with the model of Eden Court.* **Paulina** *near him.*

Leo   In the past we built cities on top of cities . . .
in the middle of cities . . .
around them . . .
Haphazard, unplanned . . . encrustations.
Layers of mistakes corrected by more mistakes . . .
Never a clean slate.
Never a clear vision.
So when they asked me to build something I thought . . .
Duty required me to . . .
I thought I had to make . . .
Because of the future . . .
A new idea. A better thing.
Look.
A thousand families . . . self-contained flats . . . connecting
walkways . . . public galleries and . . . space and . . .
structure and . . .
And the stones . . . each block represents a stone, a
monolith . . .
Do you see? Timeless.
A family in each flat.
Each block a community.
The whole estate a village.
The city encircled by estates, each one connected to the
others and to the centre.

Everything connected to the centre.
Do you see?
A design.
But it's the human element, isn't it?
Materials structure and so on . . . but the human
element . . .
Eludes you.
You can't design for it.

Paulina   Maybe they'll ask you to build the new ones.

Leo   I don't think so.

Paulina   Maybe you and Martin.
It could be a project for you.

Leo   Maybe.

Paulina   You could offer. Put in a plan . . .

Leo   No point in a plan.

Paulina   Why not?

Leo   No point in planning if anything you build can be
turned into a prison.

Paulina   Houses though, Leo.

Leo   Anything you think up can be made dangerous.

Paulina   Still. You and Martin. You could teach him. Talk
to him. Make progress.

Leo   No matter how high you build something. No matter
how well you build it. No matter how beautiful it is. You
can't build a thing high enough that if you fell off you
wouldn't hit the ground.

18

A morgue. **Martin** *sitting next to* **Billy**'s *body.* **Dorothy** *comes in.*

Dorothy   Who is he?

Martin   A friend. An acquaintance. He had my name in his pocket. That's all.

Dorothy   When you phoned . . . you sounded like you wanted someone.

Martin   Did I? I've been trying all my life to sound like that. Never managed before.

Dorothy   Is he a . . . did you . . . ?

Martin   We fucked a few times.

Dorothy   I'm sorry.

Martin   He ran off the roof of a block of flats.
Spoiled his looks apart from anything else.
His body sort of burst. He spoiled himself.
You don't get the right impression seeing him like this.

Dorothy   Do you know why he did it?

Martin   I was going to leave and he wanted to come with me. I wouldn't let him.

Dorothy   It's not your fault, Martin.

Martin   I know.

Dorothy   You mustn't feel it's your fault.

Martin   I don't.

Dorothy   Do his family know yet?

Martin   No.

Dorothy   Will you tell them?

Martin   I don't know who they are. Don't even know if he's got one. I never asked. Someone else'll tell them. There must be someone who's job it is to tell people that kind of thing.

Dorothy *goes over to hold* **Martin**.

Martin   Don't. It makes me feel uncomfortable.

Dorothy   Sorry.

Martin *touches* **Billy**'*s face. Gingerly.*

Dorothy   Do you want me to leave?

Martin   No. Stay.

Dorothy   I don't know what to say.

Martin   What effect do you want?

Dorothy   Sorry?

Martin   You want to say the right thing. What effect would saying the right thing achieve?

Dorothy   I want to comfort you.

Martin   Don't say anything then. I'll try and feel that anyway. Save you searching for words.

Dorothy   He was young.

Martin   I've never seen a dead body before. I've dreamt of it. I've thought about what it would be like. I've imagined myself dead. Everyone crowded round me. Tears etc. I've imagined you dead. Never seen it though. It's not as dramatic as I thought. It's not as beautiful. It's just Billy's empty.

Dorothy   Maybe he's in a better place. Happy somewhere.

Martin   What an ugly thought.

Dorothy   I only meant . . . we don't know.

Martin   The interesting thing is. Looking at him. Now. Me beside him. You here watching. I feel. Quite happy in a way. I feel powerful. It's almost erotic. As though for the first time I'm entitled to be . . . anything. I'm entitled to say . . . anything. To do anything. I could make a pass at you, or spit at you, or weep and you wouldn't ask me to explain, I'd be entitled.

Dorothy   Maybe.

Martin   What do you fucking mean maybe. Of course I fucking could. You'd do anything for me. You fucking worship me. You came here, didn't you? I told you to and you came, didn't you?

Dorothy   Yes.

Martin   See.
You've got that look on your face.
Tolerance.
Awe.
Fear.
When I came to the reception the woman looked at me.
She gave me that look.
I want everyone to look at me that way.
Always.
Maybe I'll have to kill you next.

Dorothy   We should leave. We're not his real family. We shouldn't be here.

Martin   You go. I want to stay.

Dorothy   Will you be long?

Martin   I don't think I ever want to move.

Dorothy *leaves.* **Martin** *looks at* **Billy** *for a while. He kisses* **Billy**. *Holds him.*

Martin   Fuck. Fuck. Fuck. Fuck.

Darkness.

19

Leo *and* **Sheena**, *in* **Leo**'s *office, studying blueprints.*

Sheena   I came to say thank you.

Leo   No need.

Sheena   I wanted to.

Leo   Where have they moved you to?

Sheena   Temporary places. Near the motorway.

Leo   Very nice.

Sheena   I've been working on the new designs.
It's a woman, the person we're working with.
You maybe know her. She does community architecture.

Leo   Probably not.

Sheena   She's very good. Helpful . . .

Leo   I'm glad.

Sheena   What are you doing?

Leo   The demolition people need blueprints so the
explosives can be placed correctly. At the points of weakness.
They need to know where the weaknesses are so they can
design the explosion. They want the structure to fall in on
itself.

Sheena   And you know where the weaknesses are?

Leo   I thought so.

Sheena   I just thought you'd put a bomb under it.

Leo   It's a complex job destroying buildings as big as this.
You can't just watch it topple. It's more clinical than that,
more surgical. The taller the building the more you need to
control it, or else the whole thing falls sideways, takes other
buildings with it, falls into the crowd. It's an interesting
operation.

Sheena   Will you be there? On the day?

Leo   Maybe.

Sheena   There'll be quite a crowd.

Leo   People love to watch things fall. The bigger the better.

Sheena   One of the kids from the estate won the
competition to press the detonator.

Leo   It's not a real detonator, you know.

Sheena   Really?

Leo   Just for show. Engineers control the process. It's all
computerised nowadays. The kid's just there for the
cameras.

Sheena   I hope nobody tells him. It'd be like telling him Santa Claus doesn't exist.

Leo   Do you still have a set of keys, Ms Mackie?

Sheena   Keys?

Leo   For your flat.

Sheena   I think so. Why?

Leo   I'd like to borrow them.

Sheena   What for?

Leo   Last look around. Take some photos. Nostalgia. Keep a record of them before they go.

Sheena   If you want. I don't need them.

She gives him a set of keys.

Leo   Thank you.

Sheena   You know, I fancy this job, Mr Black.
Do you think you can do courses?
At my age?

Leo   I'm sure you can.

Sheena   Now the campaign's finished I'm fired up for something new . . . You know. I feel . . . Do you think I'd be any good?

Leo   You've got strong ideas.

Sheena   I'd really like to do it.

Leo   You should.

Sheena   Maybe I could work for you.

Leo   I'd be happy to have you.

Sheena   That's nice of you to say.

Leo   I mean it.

Sheena   Well. I came to say thank you for what you've done.

Leo   Don't mention it.

Sheena   I know my way out.

Leo   Good luck. Ms Mackie.

20

Dorothy *and* **Joe** *in the cab of* **Joe**'*s lorry.*

Dorothy   Where are we going this time?

Joe   Glasgow.

Dorothy   What's Glasgow like?

Joe   Violent.

Dorothy   I thought Glaswegians were supposed to be friendly.

Joe   Violent but friendly. That's supposed to be the characteristic.

Dorothy   Maybe I should stay there.

Joe   Running away again?

Dorothy   I missed you. I waited for you at the side of the road but you never stopped.

Joe   I must have missed you too. Didn't see you or something. I had my eyes straight ahead. I don't often look for hitchers, you get hypnotised by the road.

Dorothy   I tried sending you dolphin calls. You mustn't have picked them up.

Joe   Maybe I did. I stopped this time.

Dorothy   What's in the back?

Joe   Who knows? It's a container. I pick up the box from the boat. Could be anything. Machinery. Grain. Meat. Metal. Anything. Could be empty.

Dorothy   You're a nice man, Joe.

Joe   Don't say that.

Dorothy   Why not? You are.

Joe   You don't know anything about me.

Dorothy   I don't need to. I can tell.

Joe   I could be a killer. Or a rapist. Maybe I pick up women and rape them in the back of the truck. Other drivers do.

Dorothy   Do you?

Joe   No.

Dorothy   Have you thought about it?

Joe   Yes.

Dorothy   You wouldn't.

Joe   That's what I say.

Dorothy   Did you miss me?

Joe   A little.

Dorothy   Do you love me?

Joe   No.

Dorothy   Could you love me?

Joe   I'll take you anywhere you want to go. I'll do anything you want me to do. I'll talk to you all night. That's better than love. You don't want me to love you.

Dorothy   How do you know?

Joe   If I loved you I'd hurt you.

Dorothy   You're a nice man, Joe.

21

The sound of dripping water. A gents' public toilet. **Martin** *stands in a urinal, a Jenners' bag next to him.*

22

Dorothy *and* **Joe** *in the truck.*

23

Paulina *potting plants.*

24

Leo *opens the door to an empty flat.*

A siren.

A voice speaks through a loud hailer.

Voice   STAND CLEAR!
STAND CLEAR!
STAND CLEAR PLEASE.
STAND WELL BACK.

The siren sounds a second time.

Leo *is alone. He looks out of the window. The sound of a crowd chanting 'ten, nine, eight, seven, six, five, four, three, two, one . . .' There is a moment of stillness.*

Darkness.

The sound of a series of explosions.

The sound of a crowd cheering and clapping.

Made in United States
North Haven, CT
24 April 2024

51739685R00114